Asset-Based Mortgage Loan Fundamentals

How Asset Depletion Mortgage Loans Work and Why Income No Longer Matters

By Joseph G. Correa

Licensed Mortgage Broker, Finibi Mortgage

Copyright & Legal Notice

Published by Live Stronger Faster

The information provided in this book is for educational and informational purposes only and does not constitute financial, legal, tax, or investment advice. The author and publisher make no representations or warranties regarding the accuracy, completeness, or applicability of the content. Readers are encouraged to consult with licensed professionals, including mortgage lenders, financial advisors, tax professionals, and attorneys, before making any financial decisions.

The strategies and examples discussed in this book are illustrative in nature and may not be suitable for all individuals or situations. Results may vary based on market conditions, lender guidelines, and individual financial circumstances. The author and publisher are not responsible for any financial losses, decisions, or outcomes resulting from the use or misuse of the information contained in this book.

First Edition, 2026

Table of Contents

Foreword

The modern mortgage world is undergoing a quiet but powerful transformation. For decades, borrowers have been conditioned to believe that income is the single most important factor in qualifying for a home loan. Pay stubs, W-2s, tax returns, and debt-to-income ratios have dominated underwriting decisions, often leaving highly capable and financially secure individuals unable to access financing simply because their income does not fit traditional guidelines. This system, while structured and familiar, fails to account for a growing segment of borrowers whose wealth is not defined by monthly income, but by accumulated assets. The Asset-Based Mortgage Mastery Series was created to bridge that gap—to introduce a new way of thinking about mortgage qualification that aligns with how wealth is actually built and maintained in the real world.

In this first book, Asset-Based Mortgage Loan Fundamentals, we begin by breaking down one of the most misunderstood yet powerful concepts in modern lending: asset depletion and asset-based qualification. This approach allows borrowers to qualify for mortgage financing based on their liquid assets rather than their earned income. It recognizes that a borrower with significant reserves—whether in savings accounts, retirement funds, or investment portfolios—can demonstrate the ability to repay a loan even without traditional employment or consistent monthly earnings. This shift represents not just a new loan program, but a new philosophy of lending—one that values financial strength over rigid documentation.

The importance of understanding asset-based mortgage loans cannot be overstated, especially in today's economy. More individuals than ever are self-employed, retired, semi-retired, or generating income through non-traditional means such as investments, business ownership, or digital assets. These individuals may have millions of dollars in assets but report minimal taxable income due to strategic financial planning. Under conventional guidelines, they are often penalized for being financially efficient. Asset-based lending changes that narrative by allowing borrowers to leverage their financial position rather than be constrained by it.

Throughout this book, you will gain a clear and structured understanding of how asset-based mortgage loans work from the ground up. We will explore how lenders calculate income from assets using asset depletion formulas, how different types of assets are evaluated, and how loan terms, risk factors, and underwriting guidelines are structured. You will learn why certain assets are considered stronger than others, how liquidity plays a role in approval decisions, and how to position yourself—or your clients—for maximum approval potential.

One of the key principles you will discover is that income, as traditionally defined, is no longer the sole indicator of a borrower's ability to repay a loan. Instead, lenders are increasingly focused on financial stability, asset longevity, and risk mitigation. For example, a borrower with $1 million in liquid assets may be able to qualify for a mortgage by dividing those assets over a set period—often 60 or 84 months—to create a qualifying "income" stream. This method reflects a more realistic view of financial capacity, particularly for individuals who live off their wealth rather than a paycheck.

Another critical concept introduced in this book is the idea of financial positioning. Asset-based lending is not simply about having money; it is about how that money is structured, documented, and presented. Two borrowers with identical net worth can receive very different outcomes depending on how their assets are allocated and how their financial profile is packaged. Understanding this distinction is what separates basic loan knowledge from true mortgage mastery. As you progress through this series, you will begin to think not just like a borrower, but like a strategist—someone who knows how to engineer approvals rather than hope for them.

This series is designed not only for borrowers, but also for professionals in the mortgage, real estate, and financial industries. Loan officers, underwriters, processors, real estate agents, and investors will all benefit from a deep understanding of asset-based lending. In many cases, the difference between closing a deal and losing it comes down to knowing which loan program to use and how to structure the file correctly. Asset-based mortgage loans open doors that traditional programs cannot, and mastering them provides a significant competitive advantage in the marketplace.

As you move through this book, you will notice that we focus heavily on clarity and practicality. This is not a theoretical discussion; it is a real-world guide designed to help you apply these concepts immediately. You will learn how to analyze a borrower's assets, determine eligibility, and understand lender expectations. You will also gain insight into common mistakes and how to avoid them—mistakes that can delay approvals, reduce loan amounts, or result in outright denials.

It is also important to recognize that asset-based lending is not a workaround or a loophole. It is a legitimate and well-established lending strategy used by major financial institutions to serve high-quality borrowers who fall outside traditional income models. These loans are underwritten with precision and care, often requiring strong credit profiles, significant reserves, and a clear demonstration of financial responsibility. In many ways, asset-based borrowers represent some of the lowest-risk clients in the market, despite being overlooked by conventional guidelines.

The broader goal of this series is to empower you with knowledge that can transform how you approach real estate financing. Whether you are looking to purchase your primary residence, invest in rental properties, refinance existing loans, or simply understand the evolving landscape of mortgage lending, asset-based strategies provide a powerful toolset. They allow you to think beyond limitations and focus on possibilities—possibilities that are grounded in financial reality rather than outdated rules.

As we begin this journey, it is essential to shift your mindset. Instead of asking, "How much income do I need to qualify?" start asking, "How can my assets work for me?" This simple change in perspective opens the door to opportunities that many borrowers never realize exist. It moves you from a position of restriction to one of control, where your financial decisions are guided by strategy rather than constraint.

In the chapters ahead, we will build a strong foundation that will support everything else in this series. You will learn the language of asset-based lending, understand the mechanics behind loan calculations, and develop the confidence to navigate this space with clarity and precision. Each concept is designed to prepare you for more advanced strategies introduced in later books, where we explore specialized applications such as retirement asset qualification, investment property financing, foreign national lending, and jumbo loan structuring.

This is more than just a book about mortgages. It is a guide to financial leverage, strategic thinking, and modern wealth utilization. It is about understanding that your financial power is not limited to what you earn each month, but expanded by what you have built over time. It is about recognizing that the rules of the game are changing—and those who understand the new rules will have a significant advantage.

Welcome to Asset-Based Mortgage Loan Fundamentals. This is where the shift begins.

Chapter 1

Understanding the Foundation of Asset-Based Mortgage Lending

Asset-based mortgage lending represents a fundamental shift in how financial institutions evaluate a borrower's ability to repay a loan. For decades, the mortgage industry has relied heavily on income verification as the primary measure of creditworthiness. Borrowers were required to provide pay stubs, W-2s, tax returns, and detailed employment histories to demonstrate stability and capacity. While this model works well for traditional employees with predictable income streams, it fails to capture the financial strength of a growing population of borrowers whose wealth is not tied to a paycheck. Asset-based lending was developed to address this gap, offering a solution that aligns more closely with how modern wealth is structured.

At its core, asset-based lending focuses on the concept of liquidity and financial reserves. Instead of asking how much a borrower earns each month, lenders ask how much the borrower has accumulated and how long those assets can sustain loan payments. This approach recognizes that individuals with substantial savings, investment portfolios, or retirement accounts often have more financial stability than someone earning a high salary with little to no reserves. The shift from income to assets is not merely a technical adjustment; it is a philosophical change in how risk is assessed and managed.

One of the key drivers behind the rise of asset-based lending is the transformation of the workforce. More individuals are self-employed, operate businesses, invest in real estate, or generate income through non-traditional means such as dividends, capital gains, or digital enterprises. These income streams can be irregular, seasonal, or intentionally minimized for tax efficiency. As a result, tax returns often do not reflect the true financial capacity of the borrower. Asset-based lending allows lenders to look beyond taxable income and evaluate the full financial picture.

Another important factor is the increasing number of retirees and semi-retirees entering the housing market. These individuals may no longer have employment income but possess significant assets in retirement accounts such as 401(k)s, IRAs, and brokerage portfolios. Traditional underwriting guidelines often struggle to accommodate these borrowers, especially if they are not taking regular distributions. Asset-based lending provides a pathway for these individuals to qualify for mortgage financing without being forced to restructure their financial strategies. To understand how asset-based lending works, it is essential to grasp the concept of asset depletion. This method involves converting a borrower's assets into a hypothetical income stream. Lenders take the total value of eligible assets and divide them over a specified period—commonly 60 months or 84 months—to determine a monthly qualifying income. This calculated income is then used in the same way as traditional income to evaluate the borrower's ability to repay the loan. The simplicity of this concept is what makes it powerful, yet the execution requires precision and a deep understanding of asset types and eligibility.

Not all assets are treated equally in this process. Liquid assets such as cash in checking or savings accounts are typically given full value because they are immediately accessible. Investment accounts, including stocks and bonds, may be subject to a discount—often around 70%—to account for market volatility. Retirement accounts may also be discounted depending on the borrower's age and accessibility of funds. Understanding these distinctions is critical, as they directly impact the qualifying income calculation and, ultimately, the loan amount.

In addition to asset evaluation, credit plays a significant role in asset-based mortgage lending. While assets can compensate for the lack of traditional income, lenders still require borrowers to demonstrate responsible credit behavior. A strong credit score indicates a history of timely payments and effective debt management, which reduces perceived risk. In many cases, asset-based loans are offered to borrowers with above-average credit profiles, further reinforcing the idea that these programs are designed for financially stable individuals.

Loan-to-value ratio is another important component of asset-based lending. This ratio represents the percentage of the property's value that is being financed. Lower loan-to-value ratios generally indicate lower risk, as the borrower has more equity in the property. Asset-based loans often require larger down payments compared to traditional loans, which further mitigates risk and aligns the borrower's interests with those of the lender. This requirement also ensures that borrowers maintain sufficient reserves after closing, which is a key consideration in the underwriting process.

The underwriting process for asset-based loans is both structured and flexible. While lenders follow specific guidelines, there is often room for interpretation and strategic positioning. This is where expertise becomes invaluable. Knowing how to present assets, document their value, and align them with lender requirements can significantly impact the outcome of a loan application. Borrowers and professionals who understand these nuances are better equipped to navigate the process and achieve successful approvals. It is also important to address common misconceptions about asset-based lending. Some believe that these loans are only available to the ultra-wealthy, but this is not necessarily the case. While higher asset levels do provide more flexibility, many borrowers with moderate savings and investment accounts can also benefit from these programs. The key is understanding how to structure those assets effectively and choose the right loan product.

Another misconception is that asset-based loans are risky or unconventional. In reality, these loans are often considered lower risk than traditional loans because they are backed by substantial financial reserves. Borrowers who qualify through assets typically have the ability to weather financial disruptions, making them more resilient in uncertain economic conditions. This stability is a significant advantage from a lender's perspective.

As you continue through this book, you will begin to see how asset-based lending fits into a broader strategy of financial optimization. It is not just about qualifying for a mortgage; it is about using your resources intelligently to achieve your goals. Whether you are purchasing a home, investing in real estate, or refinancing existing debt, asset-based strategies provide a level of flexibility that traditional lending cannot match.

This chapter serves as the foundation for everything that follows. By understanding the principles outlined here, you are preparing yourself to think differently about mortgage financing. You are moving beyond outdated models and embracing a more comprehensive view of financial capability. This shift in perspective is the first step toward mastering asset-based mortgage lending and unlocking opportunities that others may overlook.

Real-Life Math Example: How Asset-Based Mortgage Qualification Works in Practice

To fully understand the power of asset-based mortgage lending, it is essential to see how the numbers work in a real-world scenario. Imagine a borrower named Michael, a 52-year-old entrepreneur who has spent the last two decades building and selling businesses. After exiting his most recent venture, Michael decides to take time off from active work and focus on managing his investments. Although he has no traditional income, he has accumulated significant assets, including $300,000 in a savings account, $700,000 in a brokerage account, and $500,000 in a retirement account.

Michael wants to purchase a home valued at $1,000,000. He plans to put down 20%, or $200,000, leaving a loan amount of $800,000. Under traditional lending guidelines, Michael would struggle to qualify because he cannot provide consistent income documentation. However, through asset-based lending, his financial profile tells a very different story.

The first step in the calculation is determining eligible assets. Michael's savings account is fully liquid, so the entire $300,000 is counted. His brokerage account is subject to a 70% factor, reducing its usable value to $490,000. His retirement account is also discounted, typically to 70%, resulting in $350,000 of usable funds. When combined, Michael has $1,140,000 in eligible assets for qualification purposes.

Next, the lender applies the asset depletion formula. Assuming a 60-month depletion period, the lender divides $1,140,000 by 60 months. This results in a calculated monthly income of $19,000. This figure becomes Michael's qualifying income for underwriting purposes, even though he is not actively earning a salary.

With a qualifying income of $19,000 per month, the lender can now evaluate Michael's debt-to-income ratio. Suppose the estimated monthly mortgage payment, including principal, interest, taxes, and insurance, is $6,000. If Michael has minimal additional debt, his debt-to-income ratio remains well within acceptable limits. This demonstrates that his assets provide more than enough capacity to support the loan.

Another important consideration is reserves. After making the $200,000 down payment, Michael still retains a substantial portion of his assets. Lenders typically require borrowers to have several months of reserves, but in Michael's case, he has years' worth of financial coverage. This significantly reduces risk and strengthens his application.

Now consider how this scenario would differ under traditional underwriting. Without asset-based lending, Michael's lack of income would likely result in a loan denial, regardless of his net worth. This highlights the limitations of conventional guidelines and the importance of alternative qualification methods.

Let's take the example further. Suppose Michael decides to purchase a second investment property for $500,000 with a 25% down payment. Using the same asset base, the lender can recalculate his qualifying income and determine whether he can support both loans simultaneously. Because his assets are substantial, he may still qualify, allowing him to expand his real estate portfolio without returning to traditional employment.

This example illustrates the flexibility and scalability of asset-based lending. It allows borrowers to leverage their financial position in ways that align with their lifestyle and goals. Instead of being constrained by income requirements, they can use their assets as a tool for growth and opportunity.

It is also worth noting that different lenders may use slightly different calculations or depletion periods. Some may use 84 months instead of 60, which would lower the monthly qualifying income but extend the perceived longevity of assets. Understanding these variations is key to selecting the right lender and maximizing approval potential.

As you reflect on this example, consider how these principles might apply to your own situation or the clients you serve. Asset-based lending is not just a niche product; it is a powerful strategy that can open doors to new possibilities. By mastering the math behind it, you gain the ability to predict outcomes, structure deals effectively, and position yourself for success in an evolving mortgage landscape.

This is the true essence of asset-based mortgage mastery—understanding not only the concepts, but also the numbers that drive them.

Chapter 2

Types of Assets and How Lenders Evaluate Them

Understanding asset-based mortgage lending begins with a clear recognition that not all assets are created equal in the eyes of a lender. While the concept of using assets instead of income may seem straightforward, the evaluation process behind those assets is highly structured, nuanced, and strategic. Lenders are not simply looking at the total dollar amount a borrower has accumulated; they are analyzing the quality, liquidity, accessibility, stability, and risk profile of each asset category. This chapter is designed to give you a deep understanding of how different types of assets are treated, why certain assets carry more weight than others, and how to position your financial profile for maximum approval strength.

The most favored assets in asset-based lending are liquid assets. These include checking accounts, savings accounts, and money market accounts—funds that can be accessed immediately without penalty or delay. From a lender's perspective, liquidity represents certainty. Cash in a bank account is not subject to market volatility, does not require liquidation, and can be used instantly to make mortgage payments. For this reason, liquid assets are typically given full value in asset depletion calculations. A borrower with significant cash reserves is often viewed as highly stable, even in the absence of traditional income.

Closely following liquid assets are marketable securities, which include stocks, bonds, exchange-traded funds, and mutual funds held in brokerage accounts. While these assets are also relatively accessible, they carry an inherent level of risk due to market fluctuations. To account for this volatility, lenders apply a discount—commonly around 70%—to the total value of these accounts. This adjustment provides a buffer against potential losses and ensures that the borrower's qualifying income is based on a conservative estimate of asset value. Despite this discount, marketable securities remain one of the most powerful tools in asset-based qualification due to their scalability and long-term growth potential.

Retirement accounts, such as 401(k)s, IRAs, and pension funds, represent another major category of assets. These accounts are often substantial in value, particularly for borrowers who have spent decades building their retirement savings. However, they are also subject to additional considerations. Lenders must evaluate whether the borrower has access to these funds without significant penalties, which often depends on age and account structure. As a result, retirement accounts are typically discounted—often to 60% or

70% of their value—and may require documentation confirming accessibility. Even with these adjustments, retirement assets can play a critical role in qualifying borrowers who no longer have employment income.

Another category to consider is vested assets, such as stock options or restricted stock units (RSUs). These assets can be highly valuable, but they are only considered if they are fully vested and accessible. Unvested assets are generally excluded because they are contingent on future events and cannot be relied upon for repayment. For borrowers in executive or corporate roles, properly documenting vested assets can significantly enhance their qualification profile.

Cash value in life insurance policies is another asset that is sometimes overlooked but can be used in asset-based lending. Whole life or universal life insurance policies often accumulate cash value over time, which can be borrowed against or withdrawn. While not as commonly used as other asset types, these funds can contribute to a borrower's overall financial strength when properly documented.

Real estate assets, while valuable in terms of net worth, are generally not considered liquid and therefore are not directly used in asset depletion calculations. However, they can indirectly support a borrower's profile by demonstrating wealth, stability, and the ability to manage multiple properties. In some cases, equity in real estate can be converted into liquid assets through refinancing or home equity lines of credit, which can then be used for qualification.

Business ownership introduces another layer of complexity. While a business may have significant value, lenders typically focus on personal assets rather than business valuations. However, if a borrower has retained earnings or distributions that can be documented and transferred into personal accounts, these funds may become eligible for consideration. The key is ensuring that the assets are clearly owned, accessible, and verifiable.

Documentation is a critical component of asset evaluation. Lenders require clear and consistent records to verify the existence, ownership, and value of assets. This typically includes bank statements, brokerage statements, retirement account summaries, and any supporting documentation for less common asset types. The quality of documentation can significantly impact the underwriting process, as incomplete or inconsistent records can raise questions and delay approvals.

Seasoning is another important factor. Lenders often prefer assets that have been held in an account for a certain period, typically 60 to 90 days. This requirement helps ensure that the funds are genuinely owned by the borrower and not recently borrowed or transferred for the purpose of qualifying. Seasoned assets provide a clearer picture of financial stability and reduce the risk of manipulation.

Diversification also plays a role in how assets are evaluated. A borrower with a balanced portfolio—consisting of cash, investments, and retirement funds—is generally viewed more favorably than someone with all assets concentrated in a single category. Diversification reduces risk and demonstrates a more sophisticated approach to financial management, which can strengthen the overall application.

Ultimately, the goal of asset evaluation is to determine whether the borrower has sufficient, stable, and accessible resources to support the loan over time. This process requires both technical knowledge and strategic thinking. By understanding how different asset types are treated, you can make informed decisions about how to structure your financial profile and present it in the most favorable light.

As you move forward, keep in mind that asset-based lending is not just about having assets—it is about understanding how those assets are perceived, calculated, and utilized within the lending framework. Mastery comes from knowing how to align your financial position with lender expectations, creating a profile that not only meets requirements but exceeds them.

Real-Life Math Example: Evaluating and Structuring Assets for Maximum Qualification

Consider a borrower named Sophia, a 48-year-old investor who has transitioned away from active employment to focus on managing her financial portfolio. Sophia is looking to purchase a primary residence valued at $900,000 and plans to put down $180,000, resulting in a loan amount of $720,000. She does not have traditional income but has accumulated a diverse range of assets over the years.

Sophia's financial profile includes $200,000 in a savings account, $600,000 in a brokerage account, $400,000 in a retirement account, and $100,000 in vested stock options. At first glance, her total assets amount to $1,300,000. However, the lender does not use this full amount directly. Instead, each asset category is evaluated and adjusted based on its characteristics.

The savings account is fully liquid, so the entire $200,000 is counted. The brokerage account is discounted to 70%, reducing its usable value to $420,000. The retirement account is also discounted to 70%, resulting in $280,000. The vested stock options, assuming they are fully accessible, may also be discounted to 70%, contributing $70,000. When combined, Sophia's eligible assets total $970,000. Next, the lender applies the asset depletion formula. Using a 60-month period, the lender divides $970,000 by 60, resulting in a monthly qualifying income of approximately $16,166. This figure becomes the foundation for evaluating Sophia's ability to repay the loan.

Now consider her projected monthly housing expense. If the estimated mortgage payment, including taxes and insurance, is $5,200, the lender compares this against her qualifying income. With a monthly income of over $16,000, Sophia's debt-to-income ratio remains well within acceptable limits, even if she has additional minor obligations.

However, the analysis does not stop there. The lender also evaluates reserves. After her down payment of $180,000, Sophia still retains $790,000 in assets. This provides a substantial cushion, ensuring that she can continue making payments even in adverse conditions. This level of reserves significantly strengthens her application and may even lead to more favorable loan terms.

Now imagine Sophia restructures her assets before applying. She decides to move an additional $100,000 from her brokerage account into her savings account. This increases her liquid assets to $300,000 and reduces her brokerage account to $500,000. After applying the 70% factor, the brokerage account contributes $350,000 instead of $420,000, but the increased liquidity enhances her overall profile.

Recalculating her assets, Sophia now has $300,000 in liquid funds, $350,000 from her brokerage account, $280,000 from her retirement account, and $70,000 from vested stock options, totaling $1,000,000 in eligible assets. Dividing this by 60 months results in a monthly qualifying income of approximately $16,666, slightly higher than before. More importantly, the increased liquidity may improve lender confidence and streamline the underwriting process.

This example demonstrates how asset composition can influence both the quantitative and qualitative aspects of a loan application. Small adjustments in how assets are allocated can lead to meaningful improvements in qualifying income and overall approval strength.

Let's extend the scenario further. Suppose Sophia wants to purchase an additional investment property within the next year. By understanding how her assets are evaluated, she can plan ahead, ensuring that she maintains sufficient reserves and positions her portfolio to support multiple loans. This level of foresight transforms asset-based lending from a reactive process into a proactive strategy.

It is also important to consider the impact of different depletion periods. If the lender uses an 84-month period instead of 60, Sophia's monthly qualifying income would decrease to approximately $11,547. While still sufficient in this scenario, the difference highlights the importance of selecting the right lender and understanding their guidelines.

Through this real-life example, you can see that asset-based lending is both an art and a science. The math provides the framework, but the strategy determines the outcome. By mastering both elements, you gain the ability to navigate complex financial scenarios with confidence and precision.

This is the power of understanding asset evaluation—not just knowing what you have, but knowing how to use it.

Chapter 3

Asset Depletion Formulas and How Lenders Calculate Qualifying Income

At the heart of asset-based mortgage lending lies one of the most important and misunderstood components of the entire process: the asset depletion formula. This formula is what transforms a borrower's accumulated wealth into a usable, qualifying income stream. Without it, asset-based lending would not function. Understanding how this calculation works—and more importantly, how it varies across lenders—is essential for anyone seeking to master this strategy. This chapter will take you deep into the mechanics of asset depletion, showing you how lenders convert assets into income, what factors influence the calculation, and how to strategically position your assets to maximize qualifying power.

The fundamental concept of asset depletion is simple. Lenders take a borrower's eligible assets and divide them over a predetermined number of months to create a hypothetical monthly income. This income is then used in the same way as traditional employment income to determine whether the borrower can afford the mortgage. While the concept is straightforward, the execution involves several layers of adjustments, assumptions, and lender-specific guidelines that can significantly impact the final result.

The first step in the calculation is identifying eligible assets. As discussed in the previous chapter, not all assets are treated equally. Liquid assets are typically counted at 100%, while investment and retirement accounts are discounted—often to 70%—to account for risk and accessibility. Once these adjustments are made, the lender arrives at a total eligible asset figure. This number serves as the foundation for the depletion calculation.

The next step is selecting the depletion period, which is the number of months over which the assets will be distributed. Common depletion periods include 60 months (5 years) and 84 months (7 years), although some lenders may use other timeframes depending on the loan program and borrower profile. The shorter the depletion period, the higher the resulting monthly income, but the lower the perceived longevity of the assets. Conversely, a longer depletion period results in lower monthly income but demonstrates that the assets can sustain the borrower for a longer time. This balance between income and longevity is a key consideration in underwriting.

Once the eligible assets and depletion period are established, the calculation is performed by dividing the total assets by the number of months. For example, if a borrower has $900,000 in eligible assets and the lender uses a 60-month depletion period, the resulting monthly income would be $15,000. This figure becomes the borrower's qualifying income for the purposes of the loan application.

However, the process does not end there. Some lenders may subtract the down payment, closing costs, and required reserves from the total assets before performing the calculation. This adjustment ensures that the borrower is not using funds that will be depleted during the transaction to qualify for the loan. For instance, if the borrower in the previous example needs $200,000 for a down payment and $50,000 for reserves, the lender may reduce the eligible assets to $650,000 before dividing by 60 months, resulting in a monthly income of approximately $10,833 instead of $15,000. This difference can have a significant impact on loan eligibility.

Another important factor is whether the lender allows for "gross" or "net" asset calculations. Some lenders use the full adjusted asset value, while others may apply additional reductions to account for taxes, penalties, or market risk. Understanding these nuances is critical when comparing loan options, as different lenders can produce very different qualifying incomes for the same borrower. Credit and risk assessment also influence how asset depletion is applied. Borrowers with higher credit scores and lower overall risk profiles may have access to more favorable depletion terms, such as shorter periods or fewer asset discounts. On the other hand, borrowers with higher perceived risk may face more conservative calculations, reducing their qualifying income and limiting their loan options.

It is also worth noting that asset depletion is not the only method used in asset-based lending. Some lenders may allow for hybrid approaches, combining asset depletion with other forms of income, such as rental income, dividend income, or part-time employment. This flexibility can enhance the borrower's profile and increase their qualifying capacity. Understanding when and how to use these combinations is a key aspect of advanced mortgage structuring.

Timing plays a crucial role in asset depletion calculations. The value of investment accounts can fluctuate based on market conditions, which means that the timing of account statements can affect the final numbers. Borrowers and professionals who are aware of this dynamic can strategically choose when to apply, ensuring that asset values are presented at their strongest.

Another strategic consideration is the reallocation of assets prior to applying. By shifting funds from higher-risk or discounted categories into more liquid accounts, borrowers can increase their eligible asset value and improve their qualifying income. While this may not always be necessary, it can be a powerful tool in borderline scenarios where every dollar of qualifying income matters.

Documentation remains a critical component throughout this process. Lenders require clear, consistent, and verifiable records of all assets being used in the calculation. This typically includes recent statements, account histories, and any documentation needed to confirm ownership and accessibility. Incomplete or inconsistent documentation can lead to delays or adjustments in the calculation, potentially affecting the outcome of the application.

As you can see, asset depletion is both a mathematical formula and a strategic framework. The numbers provide the structure, but the strategy determines how those numbers are used. By understanding the variables involved—asset types, depletion periods, adjustments, and lender guidelines—you gain the ability to influence the outcome of your loan application in a meaningful way.

This knowledge is what separates basic understanding from

true mastery. It allows you to move beyond simply qualifying for a loan and begin optimizing your financial profile for maximum efficiency and flexibility. As you continue through this series, you will build on this foundation, learning how to apply these principles in increasingly sophisticated ways.

Real-Life Math Example: Step-by-Step Asset Depletion Calculation and Strategy

Let's consider a real-life scenario involving a borrower named Daniel, a 55-year-old semi-retired business owner who has transitioned from active income to managing his investments. Daniel is looking to refinance his current home and potentially pull out equity for future investments. His property is valued at $1,200,000, and he is seeking a loan of $700,000. While he has minimal reported income, he has built a strong asset base over the years.

Daniel's financial profile includes $250,000 in a savings account, $800,000 in a brokerage account, and $600,000 in a retirement account. At first glance, his total assets equal $1,650,000. However, the lender begins by adjusting these figures based on asset type. The savings account is counted at 100%, contributing $250,000. The brokerage account is discounted to 70%, resulting in $560,000. The retirement account is also discounted to 70%, contributing $420,000. This brings Daniel's total eligible assets to $1,230,000.

Next, the lender considers whether any funds need to be excluded for reserves or transaction costs. Since this is a refinance and Daniel is not making a down payment, the primary consideration is reserves. Suppose the lender requires 12 months of reserves, and Daniel's projected monthly housing expense is $4,500. This means $54,000 must be set aside and cannot be used in the depletion calculation. Subtracting this amount from $1,230,000 leaves $1,176,000 in usable assets.

Now the lender applies the asset depletion formula. Using a 60-month period, the calculation divides $1,176,000 by 60, resulting in a monthly qualifying income of $19,600. This figure is then used to evaluate Daniel's ability to support the new loan.

With a monthly income of $19,600 and a housing expense of $4,500, Daniel's debt-to-income ratio is extremely favorable. Even if he has additional obligations totaling $1,500 per month, his total monthly debt would be $6,000, resulting in a debt-to-income ratio of approximately 30.6%. This is well within acceptable limits for most lenders.

Now let's explore how different variables can change the outcome. If the lender uses an 84-month depletion period instead of 60, Daniel's qualifying income drops to $14,000 per month. While still sufficient, this lower figure could impact loan eligibility in tighter scenarios. This highlights the importance of lender selection and understanding their specific guidelines. Next, consider a strategic adjustment. Daniel decides to move $150,000 from his brokerage account into his savings account before applying. This increases his liquid assets to $400,000 and reduces his brokerage account to $650,000. After applying the 70% factor, the brokerage account now contributes $455,000 instead of $560,000. Recalculating his total assets, Daniel now has $400,000 in liquid funds, $455,000 from his brokerage account, and $420,000 from his retirement account, totaling $1,275,000.

After subtracting the same $54,000 in reserves, his usable assets become $1,221,000. Dividing this by 60 months results in a new qualifying income of $20,350 per month—an increase of $750 compared to the original scenario. This improvement, while seemingly small, could make a significant difference in more competitive loan situations.

Let's extend the example further. Suppose Daniel wants to purchase an additional investment property requiring a $300,000 down payment. This would reduce his available assets and require a new depletion calculation. By understanding how these numbers interact, Daniel can plan his transactions strategically, ensuring that he maintains sufficient qualifying income for both properties.

This example demonstrates the dynamic nature of asset depletion. It is not a static calculation but a flexible tool that can be adjusted and optimized based on the borrower's goals and financial structure. By mastering this process, you gain the ability to control outcomes rather than react to them.

Ultimately, asset-based lending is about leveraging what you have built. The math provides the framework, but the strategy brings it to life. When you understand both, you unlock a level of financial flexibility that traditional lending simply cannot offer.

Chapter 4

Credit, Risk, and Underwriting in Asset-Based Mortgage Lending

While asset-based mortgage lending shifts the primary focus from income to assets, it does not eliminate risk analysis. In fact, underwriting becomes even more precise. Lenders are not simply approving loans because a borrower has assets—they are evaluating whether those assets, combined with the borrower's credit behavior and overall financial profile, represent a low-risk lending opportunity. This chapter explores the critical role of credit, risk assessment, and underwriting standards in asset-based mortgage lending, and how these elements work together to determine loan approval.

The first and most important factor in this process is credit. Even in asset-based lending, credit remains a cornerstone of underwriting. A borrower's credit report tells a detailed story about how they manage debt, make payments, and handle financial obligations over time. Lenders use this information to predict future behavior. A strong credit profile indicates reliability and discipline, while a weak profile raises concerns about repayment, regardless of asset strength. In most asset-based loan programs, lenders look for higher credit scores compared to traditional loans. This is because the absence of stable income increases perceived risk, and strong credit helps offset that risk. Borrowers with credit scores in the 700+ range are often viewed more favorably, and those with scores above 740 may qualify for better pricing, lower interest rates, and more flexible terms. On the other hand, borrowers with lower scores may face stricter guidelines, higher rates, or reduced loan amounts.

Payment history is one of the most heavily weighted components of credit evaluation. Lenders carefully review whether the borrower has made timely payments on existing obligations, including mortgages, credit cards, auto loans, and other debts. Late payments, especially recent ones, can significantly impact underwriting decisions. Even a borrower with substantial assets may face challenges if their payment history suggests inconsistency or financial mismanagement.

Another key factor is credit utilization, which refers to how much of the borrower's available credit is currently being used. High utilization can signal financial stress, even if the borrower has significant assets elsewhere. Lenders prefer to see low utilization ratios, as this indicates that the borrower is not overly reliant on credit to meet their financial needs. Managing credit balances effectively is an important part of presenting a strong application. Debt obligations also play a role in risk assessment. While asset-based lending uses asset depletion to calculate income, lenders still evaluate the borrower's total monthly obligations. This includes existing mortgages, installment loans, and revolving credit payments. The relationship between these obligations and the calculated income determines the debt-to-income ratio, which remains a key metric in underwriting.

Beyond credit, lenders assess overall risk through a combination of factors. One of these is asset stability. Lenders want to ensure that the borrower's assets are not only sufficient but also stable and sustainable over time. For example, a portfolio heavily concentrated in volatile stocks may be viewed as higher risk compared to a diversified portfolio with a mix of cash, bonds, and equities. Stability reduces uncertainty, which is a critical consideration in lending.

Another aspect of risk is liquidity after closing. Lenders want to see that borrowers will retain sufficient assets after completing the transaction. This is why reserve requirements are often higher for asset-based loans. Maintaining strong post-closing reserves demonstrates that the borrower can handle unexpected expenses or market fluctuations without jeopardizing their ability to make mortgage payments.

Loan-to-value ratio also plays a significant role in risk assessment. Lower loan-to-value ratios indicate that the borrower has more equity in the property, which reduces the lender's exposure. Asset-based loans often require larger down payments for this reason. The more equity a borrower has, the more aligned their interests are with the lender, which lowers overall risk.

Property type is another consideration in underwriting. Primary residences are generally viewed as lower risk compared to investment properties or second homes. This is because borrowers are more likely to prioritize payments on their primary residence. As a result, lenders may offer more favorable terms for primary residence loans and apply stricter guidelines for other property types.

The underwriting process itself involves a comprehensive review of all these factors. Underwriters analyze the borrower's credit report, asset documentation, property details, and overall financial profile. They assess whether the borrower meets the lender's guidelines and whether the loan represents an acceptable level of risk. This process requires both technical expertise and judgment, as underwriters must interpret data and make decisions based on a combination of quantitative and qualitative factors.

Compensating factors are an important concept in asset-based underwriting. These are strengths in one area that offset weaknesses in another. For example, a borrower with slightly lower credit may still qualify if they have exceptionally strong assets and low loan-to-value. Conversely, a borrower with moderate assets may still qualify if they have excellent credit and minimal debt. Understanding how these factors interact allows borrowers and professionals to structure applications more effectively.

It is also important to recognize that different lenders have different risk tolerances. Some may be more conservative, requiring higher credit scores and larger reserves, while others may be more flexible. This variation creates opportunities for strategic lender selection. Knowing which lender is best suited for a particular borrower profile can make the difference between approval and denial.

As you move forward, it is essential to view asset-based lending through the lens of risk management. Assets provide the foundation, but credit and underwriting determine whether that foundation is strong enough to support a loan. By understanding how lenders evaluate risk, you can position yourself to meet their expectations and navigate the process with confidence.

Real-Life Math Example: How Credit and Risk Impact Loan Approval

Let's consider a borrower named Olivia, a 50-year-old investor who has accumulated significant assets but has a mixed credit history. Olivia is looking to purchase a home valued at $800,000 and plans to put down $160,000, resulting in a loan amount of $640,000. She has no traditional income but holds $900,000 in eligible assets after adjustments.

Using a 60-month depletion period, Olivia's assets generate a qualifying income of $15,000 per month. On paper, this appears strong. Her projected monthly housing expense is $4,800, which results in a favorable debt-to-income ratio of 32% when combined with her other obligations. From an asset perspective, she clearly qualifies.

However, Olivia's credit profile introduces complexity. Her credit score is 680, and her report shows two late payments in the past 12 months. While not severe, these factors raise concerns for the lender. The underwriter must determine whether Olivia's assets are sufficient to offset the perceived risk.

To assess this, the lender looks at compensating factors. Olivia has a 20% down payment, which is solid but not exceptionally high. Her reserves after closing are approximately $740,000, which is a strong positive. Her debt obligations are relatively low, and her credit utilization is moderate. These factors work in her favor.

Now consider how small changes can impact the outcome. If Olivia improves her credit score to 720 by paying down credit card balances and ensuring on-time payments for several months, her profile becomes significantly stronger. This improvement may allow her to qualify for better terms, including a lower interest rate and reduced reserve requirements.

Alternatively, Olivia could increase her down payment to 25%, reducing the loan amount to $600,000. This lowers the loan-to-value ratio and reduces risk for the lender. Combined with her strong assets, this adjustment may offset her credit concerns and lead to approval under more favorable conditions.

Let's take the example further. Suppose Olivia decides to restructure her assets to increase liquidity. By moving $100,000 into a savings account, she enhances her profile and demonstrates greater stability. This may not change her qualifying income significantly, but it improves the overall perception of risk.

Now imagine a different scenario. Olivia's credit score drops to 650 due to additional late payments. Even with strong assets, this could push her outside the acceptable range for many lenders. In this case, she may need to explore alternative programs or work on improving her credit before applying. This highlights the importance of credit as a gating factor in asset-based lending.

This example illustrates that asset-based lending is not solely about numbers. It is about how those numbers interact with risk factors. A borrower with strong assets but weak credit may face challenges, while a borrower with balanced strengths across all areas is more likely to succeed.

By understanding these dynamics, you can take control of the process. You can identify potential weaknesses, strengthen your profile, and approach lenders with confidence. This is the essence of mortgage mastery—combining knowledge, strategy, and execution to achieve your goals.

Chapter 5

Loan Structures, Terms, and Programs in Asset-Based Mortgage Lending

As you deepen your understanding of asset-based mortgage lending, it becomes clear that qualifying for a loan is only one part of the equation. Equally important is understanding how these loans are structured, what terms are available, and how different programs are designed to meet specific borrower profiles. Asset-based mortgage loans are not one-size-fits-all products. They exist across a wide spectrum of structures, each with its own advantages, trade-offs, and strategic applications. Mastering these structures allows you to not only qualify but optimize your financing for both short-term flexibility and long-term financial growth.

At a foundational level, asset-based mortgage loans mirror many of the structural elements found in traditional mortgages. Borrowers can choose between fixed-rate loans and adjustable-rate mortgages (ARMs), each offering distinct benefits. Fixed-rate loans provide stability, with the same interest rate and payment over the life of the loan. This predictability is attractive for borrowers who prioritize consistency and long-term planning. On the other hand, adjustable-rate mortgages typically offer lower initial interest rates, which can result in lower monthly payments during the introductory period. For borrowers who anticipate changes in their financial strategy—such as selling, refinancing, or reallocating assets—ARMs can be a powerful tool.

One of the most common structures in asset-based lending is the 5/6 ARM or 7/6 ARM. These loans offer a fixed rate for the first five or seven years, followed by periodic adjustments based on market conditions. The initial lower rate can significantly improve cash flow, especially for borrowers using asset depletion, as it reduces the monthly payment and improves the debt-to-income ratio. Understanding how these adjustments work, including caps and margins, is essential for evaluating long-term affordability.

Loan term length is another critical component. While 30-year terms are the most common, asset-based loans may also be structured as 15-year or 20-year terms. Shorter terms typically come with lower interest rates but higher monthly payments. For borrowers with substantial assets, a shorter term can be an attractive option, as it allows them to build equity more quickly and reduce total interest costs. However, the higher payment must still align with the qualifying income generated through asset depletion. Interest-only loan structures are particularly relevant in asset-based lending. These loans allow borrowers to pay only the interest for a specified period, typically 5 to 10 years, before transitioning to full principal and interest payments. This structure can significantly reduce initial monthly payments, making it easier to qualify under asset depletion calculations. For investors and high-net-worth individuals, interest-only loans provide flexibility, allowing them to preserve liquidity and allocate assets to higher-yield investments.

Another important structural feature is the concept of loan amortization. In a fully amortizing loan, each payment reduces both principal and interest, gradually paying down the loan balance over time. In contrast, interest-only loans delay principal reduction, which can be advantageous for cash flow but requires careful planning for the future. Understanding how amortization impacts equity, payment structure, and long-term cost is essential for making informed decisions.

Asset-based mortgage programs also vary in terms of loan size and property type. Conventional asset-based loans may have limits similar to traditional conforming loans, while non-QM (non-qualified mortgage) programs often allow for larger loan amounts, including jumbo loans. These programs are designed for borrowers who fall outside standard guidelines, offering greater flexibility in exchange for slightly higher interest rates or stricter reserve requirements. Reserve requirements are a defining feature of asset-based loan structures. Lenders typically require borrowers to maintain a certain number of months' worth of mortgage payments in reserves after closing. These reserves demonstrate the borrower's ability to continue making payments even in adverse conditions. In asset-based lending, reserve requirements can range from 6 to 24 months or more, depending on the loan program and borrower profile. Understanding how reserves are calculated and how they impact asset depletion is critical for structuring a successful application.

Prepayment penalties are another consideration. Some asset-based loan programs include penalties for paying off the loan early, typically within the first 3 to 5 years. These penalties are designed to protect the lender's return on investment. While they may result in lower interest rates, borrowers must carefully evaluate whether the restrictions align with their financial plans. For those who anticipate refinancing or selling the property in the near future, avoiding prepayment penalties may be a priority.

Closing costs and fees also play a role in loan structure. Asset-based loans may include origination fees, underwriting fees, and other costs that vary by lender. These costs can be paid upfront or rolled into the loan, depending on the program. Understanding the full cost of the loan—not just the interest rate—is essential for making a well-informed decision.

Another key aspect of loan structuring is the ability to customize terms based on the borrower's goals. For example, a borrower focused on maximizing cash flow may prioritize a lower initial rate and interest-only payments. In contrast, a borrower focused on long-term wealth preservation may choose a fixed-rate, fully amortizing loan with a shorter term. The flexibility of asset-based lending allows for these tailored approaches, making it a powerful tool for strategic financial planning.

It is also important to recognize that different lenders offer different program variations. Some may specialize in certain types of asset-based loans, such as those for high-net-worth individuals or investment properties. Others may offer more standardized programs with less flexibility. Understanding these differences and selecting the right lender is a critical step in the process.

As you continue to build your knowledge, you will begin to see how loan structure is not just a technical detail but a strategic decision. The way a loan is structured can impact cash flow, risk, tax considerations, and overall financial outcomes. By mastering these elements, you gain the ability to align your financing with your broader financial goals.

This chapter reinforces a key principle of asset-based mortgage mastery: qualification is only the beginning. True mastery comes from understanding how to structure loans in a way that maximizes opportunity, minimizes risk, and supports long-term success.

Real-Life Math Example: Structuring an Asset-Based Loan for Optimal Results

Let's consider a borrower named Ethan, a 53-year-old investor with a strong asset base and no traditional income. Ethan is looking to purchase a property valued at $1,200,000. He plans to put down $240,000, resulting in a loan amount of $960,000. His eligible assets, after adjustments, total $1,500,000.

Using a 60-month asset depletion period, Ethan's qualifying income is calculated at $25,000 per month. This provides a solid foundation for qualification, but the structure of the loan will determine how effectively he can leverage this position.

Ethan is presented with two primary options. The first is a 30-year fixed-rate loan at 6.5%, resulting in a monthly payment of approximately $6,070. The second is a 7/6 ARM with an initial rate of 5.75%, resulting in a monthly payment of approximately $5,600. Both options are viable, but they have different implications.

With the fixed-rate loan, Ethan benefits from stability. His payment remains constant, and he is protected from future rate increases. However, the higher payment slightly increases his debt-to-income ratio. With the ARM, he enjoys a lower initial payment, improving cash flow and reducing his debt-to-income ratio. However, he assumes the risk of future rate adjustments.

Now consider an interest-only option. Ethan is offered a 7-year interest-only loan at 6%, resulting in an initial monthly payment of approximately $4,800. This significantly improves his cash flow and reduces his debt-to-income ratio. With a qualifying income of $25,000, his ratio drops to under 20%, providing a strong margin of safety.

However, Ethan must consider the long-term implications. After the interest-only period, the loan will recast, and his payments will increase. If he plans to hold the property long-term, he must be prepared for this transition. Alternatively, if he plans to refinance or sell within the interest-only period, this structure may be ideal.

Next, consider reserve requirements. Suppose the lender requires 12 months of reserves based on the interest-only payment. This amounts to $57,600. Ethan's remaining assets after the down payment are $1,260,000, which easily covers this requirement. His strong reserve position enhances his application and may even allow for more favorable terms.

Now imagine Ethan wants to purchase a second investment property within the next two years. By choosing the interest-only structure, he preserves more cash flow, allowing him to accumulate additional assets and qualify for another loan. This demonstrates how loan structure can support broader investment strategies.

Let's take the example further. Suppose Ethan opts for the ARM and plans to refinance before the adjustment period. By leveraging the lower initial rate, he reduces his payments and improves his cash flow during the early years of the loan. If interest rates remain stable or decrease, he may be able to refinance into a new loan with favorable terms. However, if rates increase, he may face higher costs.

This scenario highlights the importance of aligning loan structure with future plans. Asset-based lending provides flexibility, but that flexibility must be used strategically. Each decision—fixed vs. adjustable, interest-only vs. fully amortizing, short-term vs. long-term—has implications that extend beyond the initial approval.

By understanding these dynamics, Ethan is able to choose a structure that not only meets his current needs but also supports his long-term goals. This is the essence of asset-based mortgage mastery: using knowledge and strategy to turn financing into a powerful tool for growth.

Chapter 6

Primary Residence Asset-Based Mortgage Strategies

Primary residence financing is where asset-based mortgage lending becomes most powerful for everyday application. While many borrowers initially associate asset-based lending with investors or ultra-high-net-worth individuals, its most impactful use often lies in helping individuals purchase or refinance the home they live in. This chapter focuses on how asset-based strategies are specifically applied to primary residences, how lenders evaluate these transactions, and how borrowers can structure their financial profile to achieve optimal results.

A primary residence is generally considered the lowest-risk property type from a lender's perspective. This is because borrowers are far more likely to prioritize payments on the home they live in compared to investment properties or second homes. As a result, lenders are often more flexible when structuring asset-based loans for primary residences. This flexibility can translate into higher loan-to-value ratios, lower interest rates, and more favorable terms compared to other property types. The first strategic advantage of using asset-based lending for a primary residence is the ability to qualify without relying on employment income. This is particularly beneficial for borrowers who are retired, self-employed, or in transition between careers. Instead of delaying a home purchase until income can be documented, borrowers can leverage their assets immediately. This creates opportunities to act quickly in competitive housing markets, where timing can be critical.

Another key advantage is flexibility in financial planning. Traditional mortgages often force borrowers to structure their finances in a way that maximizes reported income, sometimes at the expense of tax efficiency or investment strategy. Asset-based lending removes this constraint. Borrowers can maintain tax-efficient strategies, minimize taxable income, and still qualify for a mortgage based on their overall financial strength. This alignment between financing and financial planning is a major benefit.

When structuring a primary residence loan using assets, one of the most important considerations is the balance between down payment, reserves, and remaining assets for depletion calculations. Borrowers must ensure that they have enough assets to cover the down payment and closing costs while still maintaining sufficient reserves and qualifying income. This requires careful planning and, in some cases, reallocation of assets prior to applying. Loan-to-value ratio plays a central role in primary residence strategies. While asset-based loans may allow for higher loan-to-value ratios than investment property loans, borrowers often benefit from putting down a larger percentage. A higher down payment reduces the loan amount, lowers monthly payments, and improves the overall risk profile. This can lead to better interest rates and increased approval confidence from the lender.

Interest rate selection is another important factor. As discussed in previous chapters, borrowers can choose between fixed-rate and adjustable-rate structures. For a primary residence, many borrowers prefer the stability of a fixed-rate loan, especially if they plan to live in the property long-term. However, others may opt for an adjustable-rate mortgage or interest-only structure to reduce initial payments and preserve liquidity. The choice depends on the borrower's financial goals and time horizon.

One of the most powerful strategies in primary residence asset-based lending is optimizing cash flow. By selecting a loan structure with lower initial payments—such as an interest-only option—borrowers can reduce their monthly obligations and increase their financial flexibility. This can be particularly useful for individuals who rely on investment income or prefer to keep their assets invested rather than tied up in home equity. Another important consideration is timing. The value of assets, particularly investment accounts, can fluctuate based on market conditions. Applying for a loan when asset values are strong can result in higher qualifying income and better loan terms. Conversely, applying during a market downturn may reduce qualifying income and limit options. Strategic timing can therefore play a significant role in the success of an application.

Documentation and presentation are also critical. For primary residence loans, lenders will closely review asset statements, credit reports, and property details. Ensuring that all documentation is clear, consistent, and up to date can streamline the underwriting process and reduce the likelihood of delays or additional conditions. Borrowers who take a proactive approach to documentation often experience smoother transactions.

Refinancing is another area where asset-based strategies can be highly effective. Borrowers who initially purchased their home using traditional financing may later transition to an asset-based loan to access equity or improve terms. This can be particularly beneficial for individuals who have reduced their income over time but increased their asset base. Asset-based refinancing allows them to leverage their financial position without being constrained by income requirements. It is also important to consider long-term strategy. A primary residence is often the foundation of a borrower's financial life, and the way it is financed can have lasting implications. Asset-based lending provides flexibility, but that flexibility must be used thoughtfully. Borrowers should consider how their loan structure aligns with their long-term goals, including investment plans, retirement strategy, and lifestyle preferences.

Another strategic advantage is the ability to preserve investment capital. Instead of liquidating assets to purchase a home outright, borrowers can use asset-based financing to maintain their investments while still acquiring property. This allows them to benefit from potential market growth while leveraging low-cost financing. Over time, this approach can lead to significantly greater wealth accumulation compared to using cash for the purchase.

As you can see, asset-based lending for primary residences is not just about qualification—it is about strategy. It is about using your assets in a way that supports your broader financial goals while providing the flexibility and security needed for homeownership. By understanding these principles, you can approach primary residence financing with confidence and clarity.

Real-Life Math Example: Structuring a Primary Residence Purchase Using Assets

Let's consider a borrower named Laura, a 49-year-old investor who has transitioned away from traditional employment and now manages her wealth through a diversified portfolio. Laura is looking to purchase a primary residence valued at $950,000. She plans to put down 20%, or $190,000, resulting in a loan amount of $760,000.

Laura's asset profile includes $300,000 in a savings account, $800,000 in a brokerage account, and $500,000 in a retirement account. After applying standard discounts—100% for savings and 70% for brokerage and retirement accounts—her eligible assets total $300,000 + $560,000 + $350,000 = $1,210,000.

Before calculating her qualifying income, the lender subtracts her down payment of $190,000 and required reserves. Suppose the lender requires 12 months of reserves, and Laura's projected monthly housing expense is $5,500. This results in a reserve requirement of $66,000. Subtracting these amounts from her total assets leaves $1,210,000 - $190,000 - $66,000 = $954,000 in usable assets.

Using a 60-month depletion period, Laura's qualifying income is calculated as $954,000 ÷ 60 = $15,900 per month. This income is then used to evaluate her ability to support the loan. With a monthly housing expense of $5,500, her debt-to-income ratio is approximately 34.6%, which is well within acceptable limits.

Now let's explore how different loan structures impact her scenario. If Laura chooses a 30-year fixed-rate loan at 6.5%, her monthly payment is approximately $5,500. If she instead selects a 7/6 ARM at 5.75%, her payment drops to approximately $5,100. This reduction improves her debt-to-income ratio and increases her financial flexibility.

If Laura opts for an interest-only loan at 6%, her initial monthly payment may be approximately $3,800. This significantly reduces her debt-to-income ratio to under 25%, providing a substantial margin of safety. It also allows her to preserve more of her assets for investment purposes.

Now consider a strategic adjustment. Laura decides to increase her down payment to 25%, or $237,500. This reduces her loan amount to $712,500 and lowers her monthly payment. While this requires more upfront capital, it improves her loan-to-value ratio and may result in better interest rates. However, it also reduces the assets available for depletion, which could slightly lower her qualifying income. Recalculating her assets after the larger down payment,

Laura's usable assets become $1,210,000 - $237,500 - $66,000 = $906,500. Dividing by 60 months results in a qualifying income of approximately $15,108. While slightly lower than before, this is still sufficient for qualification, and the improved loan terms may outweigh the reduction.

Now imagine Laura wants to preserve as much liquidity as possible. She could choose the interest-only option with a 20% down payment, maintaining higher asset levels while minimizing monthly obligations. This approach allows her to keep more capital invested, potentially generating returns that exceed the cost of borrowing.

This example illustrates how multiple variables—down payment, loan structure, asset allocation, and depletion period—interact to shape the outcome of a loan application. By understanding these relationships, Laura is able to make informed decisions that align with her financial goals.

Ultimately, asset-based lending for a primary residence is about balance. It is about finding the optimal combination of assets, loan structure, and strategy to achieve both approval and long-term financial success.

Chapter 7

Investment Property Asset-Based Mortgage Strategies

As you progress deeper into asset-based mortgage lending, the conversation naturally evolves from primary residence financing to investment property strategies. This is where asset-based lending becomes a true wealth-building tool. While primary residences provide stability and lifestyle benefits, investment properties create income, appreciation, and long-term financial growth. Asset-based lending allows borrowers to expand their real estate portfolios without being constrained by traditional income limitations, making it one of the most powerful strategies available to modern investors.

Investment property lending, however, introduces a higher level of complexity and risk from the lender's perspective. Unlike a primary residence, an investment property is not essential to the borrower's daily life. This means lenders apply stricter guidelines to ensure that the borrower has both the financial capacity and the strategic discipline to manage multiple properties. Understanding these differences is critical to successfully navigating asset-based investment property financing. One of the first distinctions is the loan-to-value ratio. Investment properties typically require larger down payments than primary residences, often ranging from 20% to 30% or more. This higher equity requirement reduces the lender's risk and ensures that the borrower has significant financial commitment to the property. From a strategic standpoint, this also encourages investors to carefully evaluate each purchase, focusing on properties that align with their long-term goals.

Another key factor is reserve requirements. For investment properties, lenders often require more extensive reserves compared to primary residences. This may include 12 to 24 months of mortgage payments for each property owned, including the new purchase. These reserves demonstrate that the borrower can sustain the portfolio even if rental income fluctuates or unexpected expenses arise. For asset-based borrowers, this requirement must be carefully managed, as reserves are typically excluded from asset depletion calculations.

Asset-based lending provides a unique advantage for investment property buyers because it allows them to scale without relying on traditional income. Many real estate investors reach a point where their reported income no longer supports additional financing, even though their overall financial position is strong. Asset-based loans remove this barrier, enabling investors to continue acquiring properties based on their asset base rather than income limitations. However, this does not mean that rental income is irrelevant. In many cases, lenders will still consider projected rental income as part of the overall analysis. This can be particularly beneficial when combined with asset depletion, as it enhances the borrower's qualifying profile. Understanding how to integrate rental income with asset-based calculations is an important strategy for maximizing loan capacity.

Property type also plays a significant role in investment property lending. Single-family homes, multi-family properties, and short-term rental properties may each be evaluated differently. Some lenders have specific guidelines for certain property types, including restrictions or additional requirements. Investors must be aware of these nuances and select properties that align with lender expectations.

Cash flow analysis is another critical component. While asset-based lending focuses on assets rather than income, lenders still consider whether the property itself generates sufficient income to support its expenses. A property with strong cash flow is viewed more favorably, as it reduces reliance on the borrower's assets. Conversely, a property with negative cash flow may require stronger assets or additional reserves to offset the perceived risk. Leverage is a central concept in investment property strategies. Asset-based lending allows investors to use their assets to control larger amounts of real estate. Instead of purchasing properties outright with cash, they can use financing to acquire multiple properties, preserving liquidity and increasing potential returns. This leverage, when used strategically, can accelerate portfolio growth and create significant wealth over time.

Diversification is another important consideration. Investors who spread their assets across multiple properties and asset classes reduce overall risk. Asset-based lending supports this approach by providing the flexibility to acquire different types of properties in various markets. This diversification can enhance stability and protect against market-specific downturns.

Timing and market conditions also play a role in investment strategies. Real estate markets fluctuate, and the value of both properties and assets can change over time. Investors who understand these cycles can make more informed decisions about when to acquire, refinance, or sell properties. Asset-based lending provides the flexibility to act quickly when opportunities arise, which can be a significant advantage in competitive markets.

Another powerful strategy is the use of refinancing to unlock equity. As property values increase, investors can refinance existing properties to access equity, which can then be used to acquire additional properties. Asset-based refinancing allows this process to continue even when traditional income does not support further borrowing. This creates a cycle of growth that can significantly expand a portfolio over time.

It is also important to consider risk management. While asset-based lending provides powerful opportunities, it also requires discipline. Investors must ensure that they do not overextend themselves by taking on more debt than their assets can support. Maintaining strong reserves, monitoring cash flow, and making strategic decisions are essential for long-term success.

As you continue to build your understanding, you will begin to see how asset-based lending transforms real estate investing. It shifts the focus from limitations to possibilities, allowing investors to leverage their financial position in ways that were previously unavailable. By mastering these strategies, you can move beyond individual transactions and begin building a scalable, sustainable real estate portfolio.

Real-Life Math Example: Scaling an Investment Property Portfolio Using Asset-Based Lending

Let's consider a borrower named Marcus, a 51-year-old investor who has accumulated significant assets through business ventures and prior real estate investments. Marcus currently owns one primary residence and is looking to expand his portfolio by purchasing additional rental properties. He has $2,000,000 in total assets, which, after adjustments, result in $1,500,000 in eligible assets for asset depletion.

Marcus identifies a rental property valued at $600,000. The lender requires a 25% down payment, which amounts to $150,000, leaving a loan amount of $450,000. The projected monthly mortgage payment, including taxes and insurance, is $3,200. The property is expected to generate $3,500 in monthly rental income.

Before calculating his qualifying income, the lender subtracts the down payment and required reserves. Suppose the lender requires 12 months of reserves for the new property, totaling $38,400. Marcus's usable assets become $1,500,000 - $150,000 - $38,400 = $1,311,600.

Using a 60-month depletion period, Marcus's qualifying income is calculated as $1,311,600 ÷ 60 = $21,860 per month. This provides a strong foundation for qualification. Additionally, the rental income of $3,500 may be partially included, further enhancing his profile.

Now let's consider the impact of acquiring a second property. Marcus identifies another rental property valued at $700,000, requiring a down payment of $175,000. The projected monthly payment is $3,800, and expected rental income is $4,200. The lender now requires reserves for both properties, totaling approximately $84,000.

After accounting for both down payments and reserves, Marcus's remaining assets are reduced. However, he still maintains a substantial asset base. Recalculating his asset depletion, his qualifying income remains strong enough to support both properties, especially when combined with rental income.

This example demonstrates how asset-based lending enables scaling. Instead of being limited by income, Marcus uses his assets to qualify for multiple properties. Each acquisition is supported by a combination of asset depletion and property cash flow, creating a balanced and sustainable portfolio.

Now consider a strategic adjustment. Marcus decides to use interest-only loans for both properties, reducing his monthly payments and improving cash flow. This allows him to maintain higher reserves and potentially acquire additional properties in the future. However, he must also plan for the eventual increase in payments when the interest-only period ends.

Let's extend the scenario further. Suppose Marcus refinances his first investment property after it appreciates in value. He extracts $100,000 in equity, which he adds to his asset base. This increases his eligible assets and, in turn, his qualifying income. With this additional capacity, he is able to acquire a third property, continuing the cycle of growth.

This example highlights the dynamic nature of asset-based investment strategies. It is not a one-time transaction but an ongoing process of acquisition, optimization, and expansion. By understanding how assets, loan structures, and property performance interact, Marcus is able to build a portfolio that generates both income and long-term appreciation.

Ultimately, this is the power of asset-based mortgage lending in the investment space. It allows you to think beyond individual deals and focus on building a system—a system that leverages your assets to create lasting financial growth.

Chapter 8

Common Mistakes, Pitfalls, and How to Avoid Them in Asset-Based Mortgage Lending

As powerful as asset-based mortgage lending is, it is not without its challenges. Many borrowers and even experienced professionals misunderstand key aspects of how these loans work, leading to avoidable mistakes that can delay approvals, reduce loan amounts, or result in denials altogether. Mastery in this space is not just about knowing what to do—it is equally about knowing what not to do. This chapter focuses on the most common pitfalls in asset-based lending and provides clear strategies to avoid them, ensuring a smoother and more successful lending experience.

One of the most frequent mistakes borrowers make is overestimating the value of their assets. It is natural to look at a total account balance and assume that the full amount will be used for qualification. However, as discussed in earlier chapters, lenders apply discounts to certain asset types. Brokerage accounts, retirement funds, and other non-liquid assets are often reduced to 60% or 70% of their value. Failing to account for these adjustments can lead to unrealistic expectations and disappointment during underwriting.

Another common mistake is neglecting liquidity. Borrowers may have substantial net worth tied up in real estate, private investments, or illiquid assets, but these are not typically usable for asset depletion calculations. Lenders prioritize assets that can be easily accessed and converted into cash. Without sufficient liquidity, even a high net worth borrower may struggle to qualify. The key is to ensure that a meaningful portion of assets is held in liquid or near-liquid form.

Improper asset allocation is another critical issue. Borrowers often fail to strategically position their assets before applying for a loan. For example, keeping a large portion of funds in volatile investments may result in significant discounts, reducing qualifying income. By reallocating some of these funds into more stable or liquid accounts, borrowers can improve their qualifying profile. This type of pre-planning can make a substantial difference in the outcome of an application.

Timing is another area where mistakes frequently occur. Asset values, particularly in investment accounts, can fluctuate based on market conditions. Applying during a market downturn may reduce the value of assets used in the calculation, leading to lower qualifying income. Conversely, applying when asset values are strong can enhance qualification. Understanding market timing and being strategic about when to submit an application can significantly impact results.

Another major pitfall is failing to account for reserves. Many borrowers focus on the down payment and overlook the requirement to maintain reserves after closing. These reserves are typically excluded from asset depletion calculations, meaning they cannot be used to generate qualifying income. If borrowers do not plan for this, they may find that their usable assets are lower than expected, which can affect their ability to qualify.

Credit-related mistakes also play a significant role. While asset-based lending emphasizes assets over income, credit still remains a key factor in underwriting. Late payments, high credit utilization, and unresolved credit issues can weaken an application, even if the borrower has strong assets. Maintaining a clean and stable credit profile is essential for maximizing approval potential and securing favorable loan terms.

Documentation errors are another common challenge. Asset-based loans require detailed and accurate documentation, including account statements, ownership verification, and transaction history. Incomplete or inconsistent documentation can raise red flags during underwriting, leading to delays or additional conditions. Borrowers who take a proactive approach to organizing and presenting their documentation often experience smoother transactions.

Misunderstanding loan structures is another pitfall. Borrowers may select loan options based solely on initial payments without fully understanding long-term implications. For example, choosing an interest-only loan can reduce initial payments but may lead to higher payments later. Similarly, adjustable-rate mortgages offer lower initial rates but carry the risk of future increases. Without a clear understanding of these structures, borrowers may make decisions that do not align with their long-term goals.

Overleveraging is a significant risk in asset-based lending. The ability to qualify based on assets can create the temptation to take on more debt than is sustainable. While the math may support multiple loans, borrowers must consider the broader picture, including market conditions, property performance, and personal financial goals. Maintaining a conservative approach to leverage helps ensure long-term stability.

Another mistake is failing to work with the right lender. Asset-based lending is not standardized across all institutions.

Different lenders have different guidelines, risk tolerances, and calculation methods. Choosing a lender that does not align with the borrower's profile can lead to unnecessary challenges. Working with experienced professionals who understand the nuances of asset-based lending can significantly improve outcomes.

Communication is another area where issues can arise. Borrowers who do not clearly communicate their financial situation or fail to provide requested information promptly can slow down the process. Clear, consistent communication between the borrower, lender, and any involved professionals is essential for a successful transaction.

It is also important to avoid last-minute financial changes during the application process. Large deposits, asset transfers, or new debt can complicate underwriting and raise questions about the borrower's financial stability. Maintaining consistency in financial activity during the loan process helps ensure a smoother approval.

As you can see, many of these pitfalls are avoidable with proper knowledge and preparation. Asset-based lending requires a proactive and strategic approach. By understanding common mistakes and taking steps to avoid them, you can position yourself for success and fully leverage the benefits of this powerful lending strategy.

Real-Life Math Example: Avoiding Costly Mistakes in Asset-Based Lending

Let's consider a borrower named David, a 54-year-old investor with $1,400,000 in total assets. David is looking to purchase a home valued at $1,000,000 and plans to put down $200,000. At first glance, his financial position appears strong, and he expects to qualify easily using asset-based lending.

David's assets include $200,000 in a savings account, $900,000 in a brokerage account, and $300,000 in a retirement account. Without understanding asset adjustments, David assumes he has $1,400,000 available for qualification. However, the lender applies standard discounts, reducing the brokerage and retirement accounts to 70% of their value. This results in $200,000 + $630,000 + $210,000 = $1,040,000 in eligible assets.

David also overlooks reserve requirements. The lender requires 12 months of reserves based on a projected monthly payment of $5,800, totaling $69,600. After subtracting his down payment and reserves, his usable assets become $1,040,000 - $200,000 - $69,600 = $770,400.

Using a 60-month depletion period, David's qualifying income is calculated as $770,400 ÷ 60 = $12,840 per month. While still strong, this is significantly lower than what he initially expected. This difference could impact his loan options and terms.

Now consider another mistake. David applies during a market downturn, and his brokerage account drops by $100,000. This reduces his adjusted brokerage value by $70,000, lowering his total eligible assets to $970,000. After subtracting the same down payment and reserves, his usable assets drop to $700,400, resulting in a qualifying income of $11,673 per month.

This reduction could push his debt-to-income ratio closer to lender limits, potentially affecting approval. Had David waited for market recovery or reallocated assets into more stable accounts, he might have achieved a stronger outcome.

Now let's look at a strategic correction. David decides to move $150,000 from his brokerage account into his savings account before applying. This increases his liquid assets and reduces the impact of the 70% discount. Recalculating his assets, he now has $350,000 in savings, $525,000 from his brokerage account, and $210,000 from his retirement account, totaling $1,085,000.

After subtracting the down payment and reserves, his usable assets become $815,400. Dividing by 60 months results in a qualifying income of $13,590 per month—an improvement over his previous scenario.

Next, David addresses his credit. By paying down credit card balances and ensuring on-time payments, he increases his credit score from 690 to 730. This improvement allows him to qualify for better loan terms, including a lower interest rate, which reduces his monthly payment and further improves his debt-to-income ratio.

Finally, David selects a loan structure that aligns with his goals. Instead of choosing a higher-payment fixed-rate loan, he opts for an interest-only option, reducing his monthly payment to $4,200. This significantly improves his financial flexibility and allows him to maintain stronger reserves.

This example demonstrates how common mistakes—such as overestimating assets, ignoring reserves, poor timing, and lack of planning—can impact outcomes. It also shows how strategic adjustments can correct these issues and improve results.

By learning from these scenarios, you can approach asset-based lending with greater confidence and precision. Avoiding these pitfalls is not just about preventing problems—it is about unlocking the full potential of your financial strategy.

Chapter 9

Asset-Based Mortgage Refinancing and Equity Access Strategies

As borrowers become more experienced with asset-based mortgage lending, the focus naturally expands beyond acquisition into optimization. One of the most powerful applications of asset-based lending is refinancing—specifically, the ability to access equity, improve loan terms, and reposition financial strategies without relying on traditional income. Refinancing is not just a reactive tool used when rates drop; in the asset-based world, it becomes a proactive strategy for liquidity, leverage, and long-term wealth management.

At its core, refinancing involves replacing an existing mortgage with a new one. This can be done for several reasons: to lower the interest rate, reduce monthly payments, change the loan structure, or extract equity from the property. In traditional lending, refinancing often requires income verification, which can be a barrier for borrowers who have transitioned away from employment or who have optimized their tax strategies. Asset-based refinancing removes this barrier, allowing borrowers to qualify based on their assets instead of income. One of the most common forms of refinancing is the rate-and-term refinance. This type of refinance focuses on improving the terms of the loan, such as securing a lower interest rate or switching from an adjustable-rate mortgage to a fixed-rate loan. For asset-based borrowers, this can be particularly beneficial when market conditions change or when their financial goals evolve. By using asset depletion to qualify, borrowers can restructure their loans without needing to re-enter the workforce or alter their financial planning.

Another powerful strategy is cash-out refinancing. This allows borrowers to tap into the equity they have built in their property and convert it into liquid funds. These funds can then be used for a variety of purposes, including investing in additional real estate, funding business ventures, or consolidating higher-interest debt. Asset-based cash-out refinancing is especially valuable because it enables borrowers to access equity even if they do not have traditional income to support the new loan.

Loan-to-value ratio plays a critical role in refinancing decisions. Lenders typically limit cash-out refinancing to a certain percentage of the property's value, often between 60% and 75% for asset-based loans. This ensures that the borrower retains sufficient equity in the property, which reduces risk for the lender. Understanding these limits is essential for planning how much equity can be accessed and how it can be used effectively. Another important consideration is the impact of refinancing on asset depletion calculations. When a borrower takes cash out of a property, those funds can potentially be added to their asset base, increasing their qualifying income. However, the new loan may also result in higher monthly payments, which must be balanced against the increased income. This interplay between assets and liabilities is a key aspect of strategic refinancing.

Interest rate selection is also crucial. Borrowers must decide whether to prioritize lower rates, lower payments, or greater flexibility. For example, choosing an interest-only structure during a refinance can reduce monthly payments and improve cash flow, making it easier to qualify and maintain reserves. On the other hand, a fully amortizing loan may provide long-term stability and equity growth. The choice depends on the borrower's objectives and time horizon.

Timing is another critical factor in refinancing. Interest rates, property values, and asset values all fluctuate over time. Refinancing when rates are low or when property values have increased can result in significant financial benefits. Similarly, refinancing when asset values are strong can enhance qualifying income and improve loan terms. Strategic timing can therefore amplify the advantages of asset-based lending.

Another key strategy is portfolio optimization. Borrowers with multiple properties can use refinancing to restructure their entire portfolio. This may involve consolidating loans, adjusting terms, or extracting equity from one property to invest in another. Asset-based lending allows this process to continue even when traditional income does not support additional borrowing, creating a powerful cycle of growth.

Debt consolidation is another application of asset-based refinancing. Borrowers can use equity to pay off higher-interest debts, such as credit cards or personal loans, reducing overall interest costs and simplifying their financial structure. By replacing high-interest debt with lower-cost mortgage financing, borrowers can improve cash flow and strengthen their financial position.

It is also important to consider the costs associated with refinancing. Closing costs, fees, and potential prepayment penalties must be evaluated to determine whether the refinance makes financial sense. While asset-based lending provides flexibility, borrowers must ensure that the benefits outweigh the costs.

Risk management remains a central theme in refinancing strategies. Accessing equity increases leverage, which can amplify both gains and risks. Borrowers must carefully evaluate their ability to manage increased debt and ensure that their overall financial strategy remains sustainable. Maintaining strong reserves and a balanced asset portfolio is essential for mitigating risk.

As you continue to build your expertise, you will begin to see refinancing as more than just a financial transaction. It becomes a strategic tool for unlocking value, optimizing cash flow, and supporting long-term growth. Asset-based lending enhances this tool by removing traditional income barriers and providing greater flexibility.

Ultimately, asset-based refinancing is about control. It allows borrowers to take an active role in shaping their financial future, using their assets to create opportunities and adapt to changing circumstances. By mastering these strategies, you can transform your real estate portfolio into a dynamic, evolving system that supports your goals.

Real-Life Math Example: Using Asset-Based Refinancing to Unlock Equity and Expand Opportunities

Let's consider a borrower named Anthony, a 56-year-old investor who owns a primary residence valued at $1,300,000. He currently has an existing mortgage balance of $500,000 at an interest rate of 5.5%. Anthony has $1,200,000 in eligible assets after adjustments and is interested in accessing equity to invest in additional real estate.

Anthony decides to pursue a cash-out refinance. The lender allows a maximum loan-to-value ratio of 70%, which means he can borrow up to $910,000 ($1,300,000 × 70%). After paying off his existing mortgage of $500,000, he is able to access $410,000 in cash.

Now, let's examine how this affects his financial profile. Before the refinance, Anthony's monthly mortgage payment is approximately $2,840. After refinancing to a new loan of $910,000 at an interest rate of 6.25%, his monthly payment increases to approximately $5,600. This is a significant increase, but it must be evaluated in the context of his overall strategy.

The $410,000 in cash is added to Anthony's asset base. His new total eligible assets become $1,610,000. However, the lender requires 12 months of reserves based on the new payment, which amounts to $67,200. Subtracting this from his assets leaves $1,542,800 available for depletion.

Using a 60-month depletion period, Anthony's qualifying income is calculated as $1,542,800 ÷ 60 = $25,713 per month. This income supports his new mortgage payment of $5,600, resulting in a strong debt-to-income ratio.

Now let's explore how Anthony uses the extracted equity. He identifies an investment property valued at $800,000 and uses $200,000 from the cash-out proceeds as a down payment. The remaining $210,000 is kept as reserves and for future opportunities. The new property generates $4,000 in monthly rental income, which further enhances his financial profile.

Recalculating his position, Anthony now has two properties and a combined asset base that supports both loans. His strategy allows him to leverage his existing equity to acquire additional assets without relying on traditional income.

Let's take the scenario further. Suppose Anthony chooses an interest-only structure for the refinance, reducing his monthly payment to $4,700. This improves his cash flow and allows him to maintain higher reserves. The lower payment also reduces his debt-to-income ratio, providing additional flexibility for future transactions.

Now consider the timing aspect. If Anthony had refinanced when interest rates were lower, his new payment might have been closer to $5,000 instead of $5,600. This highlights the importance of monitoring market conditions and acting strategically.

This example demonstrates how asset-based refinancing can be used to unlock equity, increase liquidity, and support portfolio expansion. It also shows the importance of balancing increased debt with strong assets and strategic planning. By understanding these dynamics, Anthony is able to transform his existing property into a source of opportunity, using asset-based lending to build a more powerful and flexible financial position.

Chapter 10

Advanced Asset-Based Mortgage Structuring and Strategic Positioning

As you reach the final chapter of this book, the focus shifts from understanding and application to mastery and strategy. By now, you have learned how asset-based mortgage lending works, how assets are evaluated, how income is calculated, how loans are structured, and how to avoid common mistakes. This chapter brings everything together into one cohesive framework: advanced structuring. This is where asset-based lending evolves from a qualification method into a strategic system—one that allows you to engineer approvals, optimize financial outcomes, and build long-term wealth with precision.

Advanced structuring begins with a mindset shift. Instead of asking whether you qualify, you begin asking how to structure your financial profile to achieve the best possible outcome. This means looking at your assets, liabilities, credit, and goals as variables that can be adjusted and aligned. It is not about changing your financial reality, but about presenting it in a way that maximizes efficiency within lender guidelines.

One of the most powerful tools in advanced structuring is asset layering. This involves combining different types of assets—liquid funds, brokerage accounts, retirement assets, and even cash value from insurance policies—to create a stronger overall profile. By understanding how each asset type is weighted and evaluated, you can strategically allocate funds to maximize qualifying income while maintaining sufficient reserves.

Another key concept is sequencing. The order in which you execute financial transactions can significantly impact your ability to qualify. For example, purchasing one property before refinancing another may limit your available assets and reduce qualifying income. By reversing the sequence—refinancing first to increase liquidity and then purchasing—you can create a stronger position. This level of planning transforms asset-based lending into a proactive strategy rather than a reactive process.

Leverage optimization is another advanced technique. While leverage allows you to control more real estate with less capital, it must be used strategically. The goal is to balance growth with stability. This means maintaining sufficient reserves, selecting appropriate loan structures, and avoiding overexposure to market risk. Advanced borrowers understand that leverage is a tool, not a goal in itself.

Cross-collateralization is another strategy sometimes used in complex scenarios. This involves using multiple properties or asset pools to support a single loan or series of loans. While not always necessary, it can provide additional flexibility in certain situations, particularly for high-net-worth borrowers or those with diverse portfolios. However, it also introduces additional complexity and must be carefully managed.

Credit positioning also becomes more strategic at this level. Borrowers may choose to pay down certain debts, restructure credit lines, or time their applications to coincide with optimal credit profiles. Even small improvements in credit can lead to better loan terms, which can have a significant impact over the life of the loan.

Another advanced concept is income supplementation. While asset depletion is the primary method of qualification, combining it with other income sources—such as rental income, dividends, or part-time earnings—can enhance the overall profile. This hybrid approach provides additional flexibility and can increase borrowing capacity.

Tax strategy also intersects with asset-based lending. Many borrowers intentionally minimize taxable income to reduce tax liability. Asset-based lending allows them to maintain this strategy while still qualifying for financing. However, advanced structuring requires an understanding of how different financial decisions impact both taxes and lending outcomes. Coordinating these elements can lead to more efficient overall financial planning.

Portfolio-level thinking is essential in advanced structuring. Instead of evaluating each property or loan in isolation, borrowers consider how each decision affects their entire portfolio. This includes analyzing cash flow, equity, asset allocation, and risk exposure across all holdings. By taking a holistic view, borrowers can make more informed decisions and avoid unintended consequences.

Another important aspect is contingency planning. Advanced borrowers prepare for different scenarios, including market downturns, interest rate changes, and unexpected expenses. Maintaining strong reserves, diversifying assets, and selecting flexible loan structures are all part of this approach. The goal is to ensure that the financial strategy remains resilient under various conditions.

Negotiation and lender selection also play a critical role. Different lenders have different guidelines, risk tolerances, and pricing structures. Advanced borrowers and professionals understand how to match a borrower's profile with the right lender, and in some cases, negotiate terms that align more closely with their goals. This requires experience, knowledge, and a deep understanding of the lending landscape. Timing, once again, is a key variable. Advanced structuring often involves coordinating multiple transactions—purchases, refinances, asset reallocations—over time. Executing these steps in the right sequence and at the right moment can significantly enhance outcomes. This level of coordination requires careful planning and a clear understanding of both short-term and long-term objectives.

Ultimately, advanced asset-based mortgage structuring is about control. It is about moving from a position of reacting to lender requirements to actively shaping your financial profile to meet those requirements in the most advantageous way. It is about using knowledge, strategy, and discipline to turn financing into a powerful tool for wealth creation.

As you complete this book, you now have the foundation and the framework to operate at this level. You understand the mechanics, the strategies, and the potential of asset-based lending. The next step is application—taking these concepts and using them to build, grow, and optimize your financial future.

Real-Life Math Example: Advanced Structuring Across Multiple Transactions

Let's consider a borrower named Jonathan, a 57-year-old investor with a diversified asset base. Jonathan has $2,500,000 in total assets, which, after adjustments, results in $1,900,000 in eligible assets. He currently owns a primary residence with no mortgage and is looking to both acquire investment properties and maintain strong liquidity.

Jonathan's first step is to execute a cash-out refinance on his primary residence, which is valued at $1,500,000. The lender allows a 65% loan-to-value ratio, resulting in a new loan of $975,000. After accounting for closing costs, Jonathan receives approximately $950,000 in cash.

This cash is added to his asset base, increasing his total eligible assets to $2,850,000. However, the new loan introduces a monthly payment of approximately $6,200. The lender requires 12 months of reserves, totaling $74,400, which must be set aside.

After subtracting reserves, Jonathan's usable assets become $2,775,600. Using a 60-month depletion period, his qualifying income is calculated as $46,260 per month. This strong income allows him to pursue additional acquisitions.

Jonathan then identifies two investment properties, each valued at $800,000. He plans to put down 25% on each, totaling $400,000 in down payments. After these purchases, his remaining assets are reduced, but still substantial.

Recalculating his position, Jonathan's assets are now $2,375,600 after down payments. Subtracting additional reserves for both properties—approximately $90,000—leaves $2,285,600 for depletion. Dividing by 60 months results in a qualifying income of $38,093 per month.

The rental income from the two properties totals $8,000 per month, further strengthening his profile. His combined monthly obligations across all properties are approximately $12,000, resulting in a comfortable debt-to-income ratio.

Now consider a strategic adjustment. Jonathan chooses interest-only loans for the investment properties, reducing his monthly obligations to $9,500. This improves his cash flow and allows him to maintain higher reserves. It also positions him to acquire additional properties in the future.

Next, Jonathan evaluates timing. He plans to refinance one of the investment properties after it appreciates in value, extracting equity to fund another acquisition. By sequencing these transactions correctly, he maintains strong qualifying income and avoids overextending his assets.

This example demonstrates how advanced structuring brings together multiple elements—refinancing, asset allocation, loan selection, and timing—into a cohesive strategy. Jonathan is not simply qualifying for loans; he is engineering a system that supports continuous growth. By mastering these concepts, you gain the ability to operate at this level, turning asset-based lending into a powerful engine for financial expansion and long-term success.

Chapter 11

Building a Long-Term Asset-Based Mortgage Strategy for Wealth and Financial Freedom

By this point, you have developed a deep understanding of how asset-based mortgage lending works—from the fundamentals of asset depletion to advanced structuring across multiple properties. Now, the focus shifts to something even more powerful: building a long-term strategy. This chapter is about transforming everything you've learned into a repeatable system that supports wealth creation, financial independence, and long-term stability. Asset-based lending is not just a tool for individual transactions; it is a framework for designing a life where your assets work for you consistently and strategically.

The first principle of a long-term asset-based strategy is alignment. Every financial decision—whether it's acquiring a property, refinancing, reallocating assets, or selecting a loan structure—must align with your long-term goals. These goals may include generating passive income, preserving capital, growing a real estate portfolio, or achieving financial freedom. Without alignment, even the most sophisticated strategies can lead to inefficiencies or unnecessary risk. A key advantage of asset-based lending is that it allows you to decouple your financial progress from your earned income. In traditional systems, your ability to grow is limited by how much you earn and how that income is documented. In an asset-based system, your growth is driven by what you own and how effectively you use it. This shift opens the door to exponential scaling, particularly when combined with real estate investing.

One of the core components of a long-term strategy is portfolio design. Instead of focusing on individual properties, you begin to think in terms of a portfolio—a collection of assets that work together to generate income, appreciation, and stability. This includes not only real estate but also liquid assets, investment accounts, and reserves. Each component plays a role, and the goal is to create balance across the entire system.

Cash flow is a central pillar of this strategy. While asset-based lending allows you to qualify without income, sustainable cash flow ensures that your portfolio remains resilient over time. Properties that generate consistent rental income can offset mortgage payments and reduce reliance on asset depletion. This creates a self-sustaining system where your assets and investments support each other.

Equity growth is another critical factor. As properties appreciate and loans are paid down, equity increases. This equity can be accessed through refinancing and redeployed into new opportunities. Over time, this creates a cycle of growth: acquire, stabilize, appreciate, refinance, and reinvest. Asset-based lending enables this cycle to continue even when traditional income is not sufficient to support additional borrowing.

Liquidity management is equally important. While it may be tempting to maximize leverage and deploy as much capital as possible, maintaining sufficient liquidity is essential for long-term success. Liquidity provides flexibility, allowing you to respond to opportunities and challenges without disrupting your overall strategy. Strong reserves also enhance your ability to qualify for future loans and reduce risk.

Another key element is risk management. A long-term strategy must account for uncertainty, including market fluctuations, interest rate changes, and unexpected expenses. Diversification across property types, geographic locations, and asset classes helps mitigate these risks. Additionally, selecting appropriate loan structures—such as fixed-rate loans for stability or interest-only loans for flexibility—can further enhance resilience.

Time horizon plays a significant role in strategy development. Short-term decisions should support long-term objectives. For example, choosing an adjustable-rate mortgage with a lower initial rate may make sense if you plan to refinance or sell within a few years. Conversely, a fixed-rate loan may be more appropriate for properties you intend to hold long-term. Understanding how each decision fits into your timeline is essential.

Another important concept is scalability. A well-designed asset-based strategy should allow for growth without requiring constant restructuring. This means maintaining a strong asset base, managing leverage carefully, and planning transactions in a way that supports future expansion. Scalability is what transforms a collection of individual deals into a cohesive system.

Tax efficiency is also a critical consideration. Many asset-based borrowers intentionally structure their finances to minimize taxable income. This can include strategies such as depreciation, expense deductions, and deferring capital gains. Asset-based lending complements these strategies by allowing borrowers to qualify for financing without increasing taxable income. Coordinating tax planning with lending strategy can significantly enhance overall financial outcomes.

Another advanced concept is lifestyle design. Asset-based lending provides flexibility not only in financing but also in how you choose to live. Whether you prefer to travel, reduce work hours, or focus on other pursuits, your financial system can support these choices. The goal is not just to build wealth, but to create a life that aligns with your values and priorities.

Monitoring and adjustment are essential components of any long-term strategy. Financial markets, real estate values, and personal circumstances change over time. Regularly reviewing your portfolio, reassessing your goals, and making adjustments as needed ensures that your strategy remains effective. This ongoing process is what keeps your system dynamic and responsive.

Education and continuous improvement also play a role. The more you understand about asset-based lending, real estate investing, and financial strategy, the better equipped you are to make informed decisions. Staying updated on market trends, lender guidelines, and new opportunities allows you to refine your approach and maintain a competitive edge.

Ultimately, building a long-term asset-based mortgage strategy is about creating a system that works for you. It is about leveraging your assets to generate income, build equity, and support your goals over time. It is about moving from transactional thinking to strategic thinking, where every decision contributes to a larger vision.

Real-Life Math Example: Designing and Scaling a Long-Term Asset-Based Strategy

Let's consider a borrower named Carlos, a 52-year-old investor who has accumulated $2,200,000 in total assets. After applying standard adjustments, his eligible assets total $1,700,000. Carlos currently owns a primary residence with a small mortgage balance and is looking to build a portfolio of income-generating properties over the next 10 years.

Carlos begins by refinancing his primary residence to access equity. His home is valued at $1,400,000, and he refinances at a 70% loan-to-value ratio, resulting in a new loan of $980,000. After paying off his existing balance, he receives $600,000 in cash. This increases his total eligible assets to $2,300,000.

The lender requires 12 months of reserves based on a new monthly payment of $6,000, totaling $72,000. After subtracting reserves, Carlos has $2,228,000 available for depletion. Using a 60-month period, his qualifying income is calculated as $37,133 per month.

Carlos uses $400,000 of his cash to acquire two investment properties, each requiring a $200,000 down payment. The properties generate a combined rental income of $7,000 per month. After these purchases, his remaining assets are reduced but still substantial. Recalculating his position, Carlos now has approximately $1,828,000 in assets after down payments. Subtracting additional reserves for both properties—approximately $80,000—leaves $1,748,000 for depletion. Dividing by 60 months results in a qualifying income of $29,133 per month.

Carlos continues this process over several years. As his properties appreciate, he refinances to extract equity and acquire additional properties. Each transaction is carefully planned to maintain sufficient reserves and qualifying income. Over time, his portfolio grows to include six properties, generating $18,000 per month in rental income.

At this stage, Carlos's system becomes largely self-sustaining. The rental income covers his mortgage payments, while his assets continue to provide a strong foundation for additional opportunities. He has effectively transitioned from relying on asset depletion to generating income through his investments.

Now consider a strategic adjustment. Carlos decides to sell one property at a significant profit, adding $300,000 to his asset base. This increases his liquidity and allows him to reposition his portfolio. He uses these funds to acquire two smaller properties with higher cash flow, further improving his income.

This example demonstrates how a long-term asset-based strategy evolves over time. It is not static but dynamic, adapting to changing conditions and opportunities. By understanding how assets, loans, and investments interact, Carlos is able to build a system that supports both growth and stability.

This is the ultimate goal of asset-based mortgage mastery: creating a financial structure that not only meets your needs today but continues to work for you in the future, providing flexibility, security, and the opportunity for lasting wealth.

Chapter 12

Exit Strategies, Legacy Planning, and Long-Term Wealth Preservation

As you reach the final chapter of this book, the conversation evolves beyond acquisition, qualification, and growth into something even more important: preservation and exit. Building wealth through asset-based mortgage lending is powerful, but true financial mastery lies in knowing how to protect, transition, and ultimately leverage that wealth for long-term security and legacy. This chapter focuses on exit strategies, wealth preservation, and how to design a financial system that not only grows but endures across time.

An exit strategy is not something you create at the end—it is something you design from the beginning. Every property you acquire, every loan you structure, and every financial decision you make should be aligned with a long-term vision. Whether your goal is to create passive income, achieve financial independence, fund retirement, or pass wealth to future generations, your exit strategy determines how and when you transition from accumulation to preservation and distribution.

One of the most common exit strategies in real estate is the gradual payoff of debt. Over time, as mortgages are paid down and properties appreciate, equity increases and cash flow improves. Borrowers who focus on long-term ownership may choose to transition from interest-only or adjustable-rate loans into fixed-rate, fully amortizing loans, eventually eliminating debt altogether. This approach creates stability and ensures that properties generate consistent income without the burden of mortgage payments.

Another widely used strategy is portfolio consolidation. As investors grow their portfolios, they may reach a point where managing multiple properties becomes inefficient or unnecessary. At this stage, they may choose to sell certain properties and reinvest the proceeds into fewer, higher-quality assets. This reduces complexity while maintaining or even increasing income. Asset-based lending supports this transition by providing flexibility in how properties are refinanced or repositioned before sale.

The concept of timing is critical in exit planning. Real estate markets move in cycles, and understanding when to sell, refinance, or hold can significantly impact outcomes. Selling during a strong market can maximize profits, while holding during downturns may preserve long-term value. Asset-based borrowers have the advantage of flexibility, as they are not forced to sell due to income constraints. This allows them to make decisions based on strategy rather than necessity.

Another powerful exit strategy is the use of 1031 exchanges, which allow investors to defer capital gains taxes by reinvesting proceeds into similar properties. This strategy enables continued growth without immediate tax consequences, preserving more capital for future investments. While not directly tied to asset-based lending, it complements the overall strategy by enhancing capital efficiency.

Legacy planning introduces another layer of complexity and importance. For many borrowers, the ultimate goal is not just personal financial success but creating a lasting impact for future generations. This may involve structuring ownership through trusts, transferring assets to heirs, or designing a system that provides ongoing income for family members. Asset-based lending can play a role in this process by allowing assets to remain invested while still providing access to liquidity.

Tax efficiency is a central consideration in both exit and legacy planning. Strategies such as stepped-up basis, depreciation, and tax-deferred exchanges can significantly impact the amount of wealth preserved. Coordinating these strategies with asset-based lending ensures that financial decisions are aligned across all areas, maximizing overall efficiency. Liquidity management remains critical even in the later stages of a financial strategy. While it may be tempting to pay off all debt and eliminate leverage, maintaining some level of liquidity can provide flexibility and protection. Unexpected expenses, market changes, or new opportunities may require access to funds. Asset-based lending allows borrowers to access liquidity without disrupting their overall portfolio.

Another important concept is income transition. As borrowers move from accumulation to preservation, their focus often shifts from growth to stability. This may involve transitioning from high-growth investments to more stable, income-generating assets. Real estate plays a key role in this process, providing consistent cash flow that can support retirement and lifestyle needs.

Risk reduction becomes increasingly important over time. While leverage is a powerful tool for growth, it also introduces risk. As borrowers approach their long-term goals, they may choose to reduce leverage, diversify assets, and focus on stability. This transition helps protect against market volatility and ensures that wealth is preserved.

Estate planning is another essential component. This involves structuring assets in a way that facilitates smooth transfer to heirs while minimizing taxes and legal complications. Tools such as wills, trusts, and business entities can be used to achieve these objectives. Asset-based lending can support estate planning by providing liquidity without requiring asset liquidation.

Another advanced strategy is the use of refinancing as part of an exit plan. Instead of selling properties, borrowers may choose to refinance and extract equity, using the proceeds to fund retirement or other goals. This allows them to retain ownership while accessing the value they have built. Over time, rental income can continue to support the loans, creating a sustainable system.

Philanthropy is also a consideration for many high-net-worth individuals. Donating assets, establishing foundations, or supporting charitable causes can be integrated into a broader financial strategy. Asset-based lending provides flexibility in how assets are managed, allowing borrowers to balance personal goals with philanthropic objectives.

Ultimately, exit strategies and legacy planning are about intention. They require a clear vision of what you want to achieve and a structured approach to getting there. Asset-based lending provides the tools, but it is up to you to use them effectively.

As you complete this book, you now have a comprehensive understanding of asset-based mortgage lending—from fundamentals to advanced strategy. The final step is applying this knowledge to create a system that not only builds wealth but preserves and transfers it in a meaningful way.

Real-Life Math Example: Transitioning from Growth to Wealth Preservation and Legacy

Let's consider a borrower named Isabella, a 60-year-old investor who has spent the past two decades building a real estate portfolio using asset-based lending. Isabella owns five properties with a combined value of $4,500,000 and total mortgage balances of $2,000,000. She also has $1,500,000 in eligible assets after adjustments.

Her properties generate a combined rental income of $20,000 per month, while her total mortgage payments are $12,000 per month, resulting in a net cash flow of $8,000. Isabella's goal is to transition from growth to preservation, reducing risk while maintaining income.

Isabella begins by evaluating her portfolio. She identifies two properties with lower cash flow and higher maintenance requirements. She decides to sell these properties for a combined value of $1,800,000. After paying off the associated mortgage balances of $800,000, she is left with $1,000,000 in proceeds.

She reinvests $600,000 into two new properties with stronger cash flow, generating $7,000 per month in rental income. The remaining $400,000 is added to her asset base, increasing her eligible assets to $1,900,000.

Next, Isabella focuses on reducing leverage. She uses $500,000 from her assets to pay down a portion of her existing mortgages, reducing her total loan balance to $1,500,000. This lowers her monthly payments to $9,000, increasing her net cash flow to $11,000 per month.

Recalculating her asset depletion, Isabella's remaining assets after adjustments and reserves total $1,300,000. Using a 60-month period, her qualifying income is $21,666 per month. While she no longer needs to qualify for new loans, this calculation demonstrates the strength of her financial position.

Isabella then establishes a trust to manage her properties and ensure a smooth transfer to her children. She structures the trust to provide ongoing income while preserving the underlying assets. This allows her to create a legacy that extends beyond her lifetime.

Finally, Isabella considers her long-term exit. She plans to gradually refinance her remaining properties into fixed-rate loans, eliminating interest rate risk. Over time, she may choose to pay off certain loans entirely, further increasing her cash flow and stability. This example illustrates how a borrower can transition from aggressive growth to strategic preservation. By combining asset-based lending with thoughtful planning, Isabella creates a system that provides income, reduces risk, and supports her legacy goals.

This is the final stage of asset-based mortgage mastery—not just building wealth, but ensuring that it lasts, evolves, and continues to serve your vision for the future.

Chapter 13

The Future of Asset-Based Lending and Building Your Competitive Advantage

As you conclude this book, it is essential to look forward. Asset-based mortgage lending is not just a current opportunity—it is part of a larger shift in the financial world. The traditional income-based model that has dominated lending for decades is evolving, and those who understand this transition early will have a significant advantage. This chapter focuses on the future of asset-based lending, how it is likely to evolve, and how you can position yourself to stay ahead of the curve.

The financial landscape is changing rapidly. More individuals are moving away from traditional employment and toward entrepreneurship, investing, digital income streams, and flexible work arrangements. At the same time, technology is transforming how financial institutions evaluate risk, analyze data, and make lending decisions. These changes are creating an environment where asset-based lending is not just an alternative—it is becoming a necessity.

One of the key drivers of this shift is the growing disconnect between reported income and actual financial strength. Many individuals intentionally minimize taxable income for efficiency, while building substantial wealth through assets. Traditional lending models struggle to accommodate this reality, creating friction in the system. Asset-based lending addresses this gap by focusing on what truly matters: the borrower's ability to sustain payments over time.

As this model gains traction, we can expect to see increased adoption by lenders. More institutions will develop asset-based programs, refine their guidelines, and compete for borrowers in this space. This competition will likely lead to more favorable terms, greater flexibility, and expanded access. Borrowers who understand how to navigate these programs will be well positioned to take advantage of these developments.

Technology will play a major role in this evolution. Advanced data analytics, artificial intelligence, and automation are already being used to assess borrower profiles more comprehensively. In the future, lenders may be able to evaluate assets, risk, and financial behavior in real time, leading to faster approvals and more personalized loan structures. This shift will further reduce reliance on traditional income documentation and enhance the efficiency of asset-based lending.

Another important trend is the integration of financial systems. As banking, investing, and lending platforms become more interconnected, borrowers will have greater visibility and control over their financial profiles. This integration will make it easier to present a complete picture of financial strength, further supporting the adoption of asset-based lending.

Globalization is also influencing the future of lending. As capital flows across borders and investors seek opportunities in different markets, asset-based lending will play a key role in facilitating these transactions. Borrowers with global assets will increasingly rely on these strategies to access financing in multiple jurisdictions.

However, with these opportunities come new challenges. As asset-based lending becomes more widespread, competition among borrowers will increase. Lenders may also refine their risk models, introducing new requirements or adjustments. Staying ahead will require continuous learning, adaptability, and a proactive approach to financial strategy.

This is where the concept of a competitive advantage becomes critical. In any evolving system, those who understand the rules—and how to use them—gain an edge. Asset-based lending is no different. By mastering the principles outlined in this book, you position yourself ahead of the majority of borrowers who are still operating within traditional frameworks.

Your competitive advantage comes from several factors. First, knowledge. Understanding how asset-based lending works, how assets are evaluated, and how loans are structured allows you to make informed decisions. Second, strategy. Knowing how to align your financial profile with lender expectations enables you to achieve better outcomes. Third, execution. Taking action at the right time, with the right structure, ensures that your strategy translates into results.

Another key component is adaptability. The financial world will continue to change, and the ability to adjust your strategy accordingly is essential. This may involve reallocating assets, exploring new loan programs, or adjusting your portfolio based on market conditions. Flexibility is one of the greatest strengths of asset-based lending, and it should be reflected in your approach.

Networking and relationships also play a role. Working with experienced lenders, brokers, and financial professionals who understand asset-based lending can provide valuable insights and opportunities. These relationships can help you navigate complex scenarios, access specialized programs, and stay informed about industry developments.

Education should be an ongoing process. The more you learn, the more effectively you can apply these strategies. This includes not only lending but also real estate, investing, tax planning, and financial management. A well-rounded understanding enhances your ability to make strategic decisions and maintain your competitive edge.

Another important aspect is mindset. Asset-based lending requires a shift in how you think about money and opportunity. Instead of focusing on limitations, you focus on possibilities. Instead of asking what you can afford based on income, you ask how your assets can be leveraged to achieve your goals. This mindset is what drives innovation and success.

As you look to the future, consider how you can build a system that evolves with you. Your financial strategy should not be static. It should grow, adapt, and improve over time. Asset-based lending provides the flexibility to make this possible, allowing you to adjust your approach as your goals and circumstances change.

It is also important to think about scalability. The strategies you use today should support your ability to expand in the future. This means maintaining strong assets, managing leverage carefully, and planning transactions in a way that preserves flexibility. Scalability is what allows you to move from individual opportunities to sustained growth.

Another forward-looking consideration is innovation. New financial products, technologies, and strategies will continue to emerge. Being open to these innovations—and understanding how they fit into your overall strategy—can provide additional opportunities. Asset-based lending itself is an example of innovation, and it will continue to evolve.

Ultimately, the future of asset-based lending is about alignment with how wealth is actually created and managed. It reflects a shift toward a more accurate and flexible understanding of financial strength. By embracing this shift, you position yourself not just to participate in the system, but to excel within it.

Real-Life Math Example: Positioning for Future Growth and Competitive Advantage

Let's consider a borrower named Victor, a 48-year-old entrepreneur who has built a diversified asset base of $1,800,000. After adjustments, his eligible assets total $1,350,000. Victor is planning for the next phase of his financial journey, focusing on growth, flexibility, and long-term positioning.

Victor begins by purchasing a primary residence valued at $900,000 with a 20% down payment of $180,000. His loan amount is $720,000, and his monthly payment is approximately $5,200. After subtracting the down payment and required reserves of $62,400, his remaining assets are $1,107,600. Using a 60-month depletion period, Victor's qualifying income is calculated as $18,460 per month. This supports his current loan comfortably and positions him for future opportunities.

Victor then identifies an investment property valued at $650,000, requiring a down payment of $162,500. After this purchase, his remaining assets are reduced, but still sufficient for further transactions. The property generates $3,200 in monthly rental income, which enhances his overall financial profile.

Recalculating his asset depletion, Victor's qualifying income remains strong enough to support both properties. He now has a system in place that combines asset-based qualification with rental income, creating a balanced approach.

Looking ahead, Victor plans to leverage technology and market trends. He monitors asset values, interest rates, and new lending programs, positioning himself to act when opportunities arise. For example, if interest rates decrease, he may refinance to lower his payments and improve cash flow.

Victor also focuses on maintaining liquidity. Instead of deploying all his assets, he keeps a portion in liquid accounts, ensuring that he can respond to new opportunities or challenges. This flexibility becomes a key part of his competitive advantage. Now consider a future scenario. Victor's investment property appreciates to $800,000, and he refinances at a 70% loan-to-value ratio, extracting additional equity. This increases his asset base and allows him to acquire another property, continuing the cycle of growth.

Through careful planning, strategic execution, and continuous learning, Victor builds a system that evolves with him. He is not limited by traditional income constraints but empowered by his understanding of asset-based lending.

This example illustrates how positioning, strategy, and adaptability create a competitive advantage. By applying these principles, you can navigate the future of asset-based lending with confidence and precision, turning knowledge into lasting opportunity.

Chapter 14

Creating Your Personal Asset-Based Mortgage Blueprint

By the time you reach this stage, you are no longer simply learning about asset-based mortgage lending—you are ready to design your own system. This chapter is about turning everything you've learned into a personalized blueprint. A blueprint is not just a plan; it is a structured, repeatable framework that guides your financial decisions over time. It allows you to move with clarity, confidence, and consistency, regardless of changing market conditions or personal circumstances.

The first step in building your blueprint is clarity of vision. You must define what you are working toward. For some, the goal may be passive income and early financial independence. For others, it may be long-term wealth preservation, portfolio growth, or legacy planning. Without a clear destination, even the most sophisticated strategies can become scattered and ineffective. Your blueprint begins with a simple but powerful question: What do you want your financial life to look like in 5, 10, or 20 years? Once your vision is clear, the next step is assessing your current position. This involves taking a detailed inventory of your assets, liabilities, credit profile, and existing properties. You must understand not only what you have, but how it is structured. How much of your wealth is liquid? How much is tied up in investments or real estate? What are your current obligations? This assessment provides the foundation for your blueprint and highlights areas that may need adjustment.

Asset allocation becomes a central focus at this stage. As you have learned, not all assets are treated equally in asset-based lending. Your blueprint should include a strategic allocation of funds across liquid accounts, investment portfolios, and other asset categories. The goal is to maximize both qualifying income and financial flexibility. This may involve reallocating assets to improve liquidity or reduce volatility, depending on your objectives.

Next, you must define your acquisition strategy. This includes determining what types of properties you want to acquire, how frequently you plan to purchase, and how each acquisition fits into your overall system. Some borrowers focus on primary residences and lifestyle optimization, while others prioritize investment properties and cash flow. Your blueprint should clearly outline your approach, including target price ranges, property types, and geographic areas. Loan structuring is another critical component. Based on your goals, you must decide which types of loans align with your strategy. Fixed-rate loans may provide stability for long-term holdings, while adjustable-rate or interest-only loans may offer flexibility and improved cash flow. Your blueprint should include guidelines for selecting loan structures based on different scenarios, ensuring that each decision supports your broader objectives.

Cash flow management is a key pillar of your blueprint. Even though asset-based lending allows you to qualify without traditional income, sustainable cash flow is essential for long-term success. Your plan should include strategies for balancing asset depletion with rental income, ensuring that your system remains resilient over time. This may involve prioritizing properties with strong cash flow or structuring loans to minimize monthly obligations.

Reserve management is equally important. Your blueprint should define how much liquidity you maintain at all times and how reserves are replenished after each transaction. Strong reserves not only support loan approvals but also provide a safety net for unexpected events. This is a non-negotiable element of any successful asset-based strategy.

Another essential component is sequencing. The order in which you execute transactions—purchases, refinances, asset reallocations—can significantly impact your ability to qualify and grow. Your blueprint should include a clear framework for sequencing decisions, ensuring that each step strengthens your position rather than limiting it. For example, refinancing to increase liquidity before acquiring new properties can enhance your overall capacity.

Risk management must also be integrated into your blueprint. This includes setting limits on leverage, diversifying assets, and preparing for potential market changes. Your strategy should account for different scenarios, including economic downturns or changes in interest rates. By planning for these possibilities, you create a system that is both flexible and resilient.

Another key element is scalability. Your blueprint should be designed to grow with you. This means maintaining sufficient assets, managing debt carefully, and structuring transactions in a way that preserves future opportunities. A scalable system allows you to expand without constantly needing to restructure or reset your approach.

Tax efficiency should also be considered. Coordinating your asset-based lending strategy with tax planning can significantly enhance your overall results. This may involve working with professionals to align your investment, lending, and tax strategies in a cohesive way.

Monitoring and adjustment are ongoing components of your blueprint. Your financial system is not static—it evolves over time. Regularly reviewing your portfolio, reassessing your goals, and making adjustments ensures that your strategy remains aligned with your objectives. This process turns your blueprint into a living system rather than a fixed plan.

Another important aspect is discipline. Having a blueprint is only valuable if you follow it. This requires consistency in decision-making and the ability to avoid impulsive actions that do not align with your strategy. Discipline is what transforms knowledge into results.

Finally, your blueprint should reflect your personal values and lifestyle. Financial success is not just about numbers—it is about creating a life that aligns with what matters to you. Whether that means flexibility, security, or growth, your blueprint should support your vision for how you want to live.

By the end of this chapter, you should see that asset-based mortgage lending is not just a tool—it is a system. And your blueprint is the framework that allows you to use that system effectively. It is your roadmap, your strategy, and your guide for building long-term financial success.

Real-Life Math Example: Designing and Executing a Personal Asset-Based Blueprint

Let's consider a borrower named Daniel, a 50-year-old investor with $1,600,000 in total assets. After adjustments, his eligible assets total $1,200,000. Daniel's goal is to build a portfolio of three to four properties over the next five years while maintaining strong liquidity and minimizing risk.

Daniel begins by purchasing a primary residence valued at $850,000. He puts down 20%, or $170,000, resulting in a loan amount of $680,000. His monthly payment is approximately $4,800. After subtracting his down payment and required reserves of $57,600, his remaining assets are $972,400.

Using a 60-month depletion period, Daniel's qualifying income is calculated as $16,206 per month. This supports his current loan and provides a foundation for future acquisitions.

Next, Daniel follows his blueprint and acquires an investment property valued at $600,000, with a 25% down payment of $150,000. The property generates $3,000 in monthly rental income. After this purchase, his remaining assets are reduced, but still sufficient.

Recalculating his position, Daniel's assets are now approximately $822,400. Subtracting additional reserves for the new property—approximately $36,000—leaves $786,400 for depletion. Dividing by 60 months results in a qualifying income of $13,106 per month. Daniel then evaluates his next step. Based on his blueprint, he decides to wait for his assets to grow before acquiring another property. Over the next year, his investments increase in value, adding $100,000 to his asset base. This improves his qualifying income and positions him for the next acquisition.

He then purchases a second investment property valued at $700,000, following the same structure. With each step, Daniel adheres to his blueprint, ensuring that he maintains sufficient reserves and aligns each decision with his long-term goals.

Now consider a strategic adjustment. Daniel chooses an interest-only loan for his second investment property, reducing his monthly payment and improving cash flow. This allows him to maintain higher reserves and prepares him for future opportunities.

Over time, Daniel's system begins to take shape. His properties generate rental income, his assets continue to grow, and his blueprint guides each decision. He is no longer reacting to opportunities—he is creating them.

This example demonstrates how a personal blueprint

transforms asset-based lending into a structured, repeatable system. By following a clear plan, Daniel is able to build a portfolio that aligns with his goals, maintains flexibility, and supports long-term success. This is the ultimate objective of this book: not just to teach you how asset-based lending works, but to empower you to design and execute your own strategy with confidence and precision.

Chapter 15

Becoming the Bank — Turning Asset-Based Lending Into Your Own Financing System

At the highest level of financial strategy, the goal is no longer just to qualify for loans or build a portfolio—it is to control capital. This is where asset-based mortgage mastery evolves into something far more powerful: becoming the bank. This concept represents a shift from being a borrower within the system to operating with the same principles that lenders use to create, deploy, and recycle capital. It is the ultimate form of financial leverage and control, and it is fully aligned with everything you have learned throughout this book.

When you understand how lenders think, structure loans, and manage risk, you begin to realize that the same principles can be applied to your own financial system. Banks do not rely on income in the same way individuals do. They operate based on assets, liquidity, and the strategic deployment of capital. Asset-based lending gives you access to these same principles, allowing you to think and operate like a lender rather than a traditional borrower. The foundation of becoming the bank is liquidity and control. Instead of tying up all your capital in properties, you maintain access to funds that can be deployed quickly and efficiently. This may involve using asset-based refinancing, lines of credit, or other financial tools to create a pool of capital that can be used for investments, opportunities, or even lending to others.

One of the key strategies in this approach is capital recycling. Instead of using your own cash for each purchase, you use financing to acquire assets, allow those assets to appreciate, and then refinance to extract equity. This equity is then redeployed into new opportunities. Over time, this creates a cycle where your capital is continuously working, expanding your portfolio without requiring additional income.

Another important concept is yield optimization. As you build your financial system, you begin to evaluate opportunities based on returns. This includes not only real estate but also other investments or lending opportunities. For example, you may choose to lend money to other investors at a higher interest rate than your own borrowing cost, effectively creating a spread. This is the same principle that banks use to generate profit.

Private lending is one of the most direct ways to become the bank. By using your assets to secure low-cost financing, you can lend capital to others at higher rates, generating income while maintaining control of your underlying assets. This strategy requires careful risk management, but it can be highly effective when executed properly.

Another advanced strategy is the use of lines of credit, such as home equity lines or securities-backed lines. These tools provide flexible access to capital without requiring a full refinance. This allows you to act quickly when opportunities arise, whether it is acquiring a property, funding a deal, or investing in another asset.

Risk management becomes even more critical at this level. As you begin to operate like a lender, you must evaluate not only your own risk but also the risk of others. This includes assessing collateral, borrower profiles, and market conditions. Maintaining strong reserves and avoiding overexposure are essential for long-term success.

Another key element is control over timing. When you have access to capital, you are no longer dependent on external approval for every opportunity. This allows you to move quickly, negotiate better terms, and take advantage of situations that others may miss. Timing becomes a strategic advantage rather than a constraint.

Tax efficiency also plays a role in this strategy. By using debt strategically, you can preserve your assets while still accessing liquidity. This allows you to maintain investments that continue to grow while using borrowed funds for new opportunities. Coordinating this approach with tax planning can enhance overall returns.

Another important concept is scalability. As you build your system, you can expand beyond individual transactions and begin operating at a portfolio level. This includes managing multiple properties, loans, and investments in a coordinated way. The goal is to create a system that grows over time, with each component supporting the others.

Mindset is perhaps the most important factor. Becoming the bank requires a shift in how you think about money, risk, and opportunity. Instead of focusing on limitations, you focus on structure. Instead of asking whether you can afford something, you ask how to structure it. This mindset opens the door to new possibilities and allows you to operate at a higher level.

It is also important to recognize that this approach is not about taking unnecessary risk. It is about using leverage intelligently, maintaining control, and making decisions that align with your long-term goals. Discipline, planning, and continuous learning are essential components of this process.

As you move forward, consider how you can integrate these principles into your own financial system. Whether it is through refinancing, private lending, or strategic investing, the goal is to create a structure that allows your capital to work for you continuously.

This is the final evolution of asset-based mortgage mastery. It is not just about using the system—it is about becoming part of it, understanding it at a deeper level, and using it to create lasting financial power.

Real-Life Math Example: Building a Personal Lending System Using Asset-Based Strategies

Let's consider a borrower named Robert, a 55-year-old investor with $2,000,000 in total assets. After adjustments, his eligible assets total $1,500,000. Robert owns two properties with a combined value of $2,200,000 and total mortgage balances of $900,000.

Robert begins by refinancing one of his properties to access equity. The property is valued at $1,200,000, and he refinances at a 70% loan-to-value ratio, resulting in a new loan of $840,000. After paying off his existing balance of $400,000, he receives $440,000 in cash.

This cash is added to his asset base, increasing his eligible assets to $1,940,000. After subtracting reserves of $60,000, his usable assets are $1,880,000. Using a 60-month depletion period, his qualifying income is calculated as $31,333 per month.

Robert decides to allocate $300,000 of this capital to private lending. He lends this amount to another investor at an interest rate of 10%, generating $30,000 per year in interest income, or $2,500 per month. His own borrowing cost on the refinanced loan is 6%, creating a positive spread.

The remaining $140,000 is used as a down payment on an investment property valued at $560,000. This property generates $3,200 in monthly rental income. Robert now has multiple income streams: rental income, interest income, and asset-based qualifying income.

Recalculating his position, Robert's system becomes more robust. His assets support his loans, his properties generate income, and his lending activities create additional returns. Each component reinforces the others.

Now consider scalability. As Robert continues to refinance properties and reinvest capital, his lending pool grows. He may increase his private lending to $500,000, generating $50,000 per year in interest income. At the same time, his real estate portfolio continues to expand.

This example demonstrates how asset-based lending can be

used not just to acquire properties, but to create a complete financial system. By understanding and applying these principles, Robert transitions from being a borrower to operating like a lender.

This is the highest level of strategy—where your assets, loans, and investments work together to create continuous growth, income, and opportunity.

Final Thoughts

Mastery, Freedom, and the Power of Strategic Financial Thinking

As you reach the end of this book, it is important to pause and recognize how much your perspective has likely shifted. What began as an exploration of an alternative mortgage strategy has evolved into something far more powerful—a complete transformation in how you view money, assets, and opportunity. Asset-based mortgage lending is not just a niche product or a workaround for unconventional borrowers. It is a framework for thinking differently, acting strategically, and building a life that is not constrained by traditional financial limitations.

For most people, the financial system has always revolved around income. From the moment you begin working, everything is measured by how much you earn, how stable that income is, and how it fits into predefined guidelines. This model has dominated lending, investing, and financial planning for decades. But as you have seen throughout this book, this model is no longer sufficient for the realities of today's economy. Wealth is no longer defined solely by income—it is defined by assets, by ownership, and by the ability to leverage what you have built over time. This is the central idea that underpins everything you have learned: your financial power is not limited to what you earn each month. It is expanded by what you accumulate, how you structure it, and how effectively you use it. Asset-based mortgage lending simply brings this reality into focus, allowing you to operate within a system that recognizes and rewards true financial strength.

One of the most important takeaways from this journey is the concept of control. Traditional lending often places borrowers in a reactive position, where they must meet rigid requirements and adjust their lives to fit the system. Asset-based lending, when understood and applied correctly, shifts that dynamic. It allows you to take a proactive role in shaping your financial profile, structuring your assets, and making decisions that align with your goals. This shift from reactive to proactive thinking is where true mastery begins.

Another critical insight is the importance of strategy over transactions. Throughout this book, you have seen how individual decisions—whether it's choosing a loan structure, reallocating assets, or timing a refinance—can have a significant impact on outcomes. But the real power comes from connecting these decisions into a larger strategy. When you begin to think in terms of systems rather than isolated actions, you unlock a level of efficiency and scalability that is not possible otherwise. This is especially true in real estate. Property ownership, when combined with asset-based lending, becomes more than just an investment—it becomes a platform. A platform for generating income, building equity, accessing liquidity, and creating opportunities. Each property, each loan, and each asset becomes a component of a larger system designed to support your financial vision.

It is also important to recognize that with greater flexibility comes greater responsibility. Asset-based lending provides powerful tools, but those tools must be used wisely. Overleveraging, poor planning, or lack of discipline can undermine even the strongest financial position. The goal is not simply to qualify for more, but to build sustainably. To create a system that can withstand changes in markets, interest rates, and personal circumstances.

This is where the principles of balance and risk management come into play. Maintaining adequate reserves, diversifying assets, and aligning loan structures with your time horizon are not just best practices—they are essential components of long-term success. The most successful borrowers are not those who take the most risk, but those who understand how to manage it effectively.

Another theme that has emerged throughout this book is the importance of timing. Financial decisions do not exist in a vacuum. Market conditions, asset values, interest rates, and personal circumstances all influence outcomes. Being aware of these factors and acting strategically can amplify results. This does not mean trying to predict the future with certainty, but rather positioning yourself to take advantage of opportunities when they arise.

Education and awareness are also key. The more you understand about how asset-based lending works, the more effectively you can use it. This includes not only the technical aspects—such as asset depletion calculations and loan structures—but also the broader financial landscape. Staying informed allows you to adapt, refine your strategy, and continue growing over time.

As you move forward, it is important to remember that this knowledge is not static. The financial world continues to evolve, and new opportunities will emerge. Asset-based lending itself will continue to develop, with new programs, guidelines, and strategies. By maintaining a mindset of continuous learning, you ensure that you remain ahead of the curve.

Perhaps the most powerful aspect of everything you have learned is the ability to design your own financial path. Instead of following a predetermined route based on income and employment, you now have the tools to create a system that reflects your unique goals and circumstances. Whether that means building a real estate portfolio, preserving wealth for future generations, or creating a lifestyle of flexibility and freedom, the choice is yours.

This is where the concept of financial freedom becomes tangible. It is not just about having money—it is about having options. Options to invest, to travel, to spend time with family, to pursue passions, and to make decisions without being constrained by financial limitations. Asset-based lending, when used strategically, can be a powerful vehicle for achieving this level of freedom.

Legacy is another important consideration. The systems you build today have the potential to extend beyond your lifetime, providing opportunities and security for future generations. By structuring your assets, properties, and financial strategies thoughtfully, you can create a lasting impact that goes far beyond individual transactions.

As you reflect on everything covered in this book, it is worth considering how you will apply these principles in your own life. Knowledge alone is not enough—action is what creates results. Start by evaluating your current financial position. Identify your assets, understand how they are structured, and consider how they can be optimized. Look at your goals and begin to align your strategy accordingly.

You do not need to implement everything at once. In fact, the most effective approach is often incremental. Small, strategic decisions made consistently over time can lead to significant results. Whether it is reallocating assets, exploring new loan options, or planning your next investment, each step moves you closer to your objectives.

It is also important to surround yourself with the right team. Asset-based lending often involves multiple professionals, including lenders, financial advisors, and real estate experts. Working with individuals who understand this space and can support your strategy can make a substantial difference in your outcomes.

Finally, remember that mastery is a process, not a destination. The concepts you have learned here provide a foundation, but true mastery comes from application, experience, and continuous refinement. Each transaction, each decision, and each outcome adds to your understanding and strengthens your ability to navigate this space.

You now have the knowledge to think differently, to act strategically, and to use your assets as a powerful tool for growth and opportunity. The question is not whether you can apply these principles—it is how far you are willing to take them.

This is the beginning of a new way of operating. A way that is not limited by traditional rules, but guided by strategy, discipline, and vision. A way that allows you to take control of your financial future and build something that is not only successful, but sustainable and meaningful.

The system is there. The tools are in your hands. The next move is yours.

How to Get a Personalized Asset-Based Mortgage Review

If you found *Asset-Based Mortgage Loan Fundamentals: How Asset Depletion Mortgage Loans Work and Why Income No Longer Matters* helpful, you may want to see how these concepts apply to your specific financial situation. Asset-based lending is highly customized—your assets, liquidity, credit profile, property type, and long-term goals all play a role in determining what you qualify for and how your loan should be structured.

Every borrower's situation is different. The type of assets you hold, how those assets are allocated, your credit history, the property you are purchasing or refinancing, and current lender guidelines all affect your options. The strategies and examples in this book are designed to teach you how asset-based mortgage loans work—but your actual qualifying income, loan amount, and structure can only be determined by reviewing your real numbers.

If you would like a no-obligation Asset-Based Mortgage review, you can request one here:

Email: **info@FinibiMortgage.com**

A licensed mortgage broker will review your assets, credit profile, and goals, and explain what asset-based mortgage options may be available to you—including asset depletion loans, investment property financing, refinancing strategies, and advanced structuring approaches tailored to your situation.

No cost. No pressure. No obligation.

Sincerely,

Joseph G. Correa

Finibi Mortgage Inc.

Licensed Mortgage Broker

About the Author

Joseph G. Correa is a licensed mortgage broker and the founder of Finibi Mortgage, a Florida-based brokerage specializing in asset-based mortgage lending, alternative financing, and strategic real estate funding solutions for homeowners, investors, and high-net-worth borrowers. With more than two decades of experience in mortgage lending, underwriting, and financial structuring, Joseph has helped thousands of clients qualify for real estate using assets instead of traditional income, unlocking opportunities that conventional lending often restricts.

Unlike traditional loan officers who focus solely on income-based approvals, Joseph's approach is centered on asset positioning, financial strategy, and long-term wealth building. He believes that mortgages should not be limited by outdated income rules, but instead structured around true financial strength—assets, liquidity, and intelligent leverage. This philosophy has made him a trusted advisor for entrepreneurs, retirees, self-employed individuals, and investors who need flexible financing solutions that align with how they actually build and manage wealth.

Joseph is widely recognized for his expertise in asset depletion mortgage loans, bank statement programs, non-QM lending, investment property financing, and advanced structuring strategies that allow borrowers to qualify without relying on tax returns or W-2 income. His ability to simplify complex underwriting guidelines into clear, actionable strategies has helped clients use their savings, investment portfolios, and retirement accounts to acquire real estate, scale portfolios, and preserve liquidity.

Through his education platform, Finibi Academy, Joseph has trained tens of thousands of students worldwide in mortgage strategy, credit optimization, real estate investing, and financial independence. His courses and books are designed for both beginners and experienced professionals who want a deeper understanding of how modern lending truly works beyond traditional income-based limitations.

Joseph created The Asset-Based Mortgage Mastery Series to provide a clear, practical roadmap for borrowers and professionals who want to leverage assets instead of income to qualify for real estate. His mission is simple: to help people understand how to use their assets as a powerful financial tool, eliminate unnecessary barriers to financing, and build long-term wealth through strategic lending.

When he is not structuring loans or writing, Joseph works with clients across the United States to design customized asset-based mortgage strategies that align with their financial goals, liquidity needs, and long-term investment plans.

The Asset-Based Mortgage Mastery Series Roadmap

The Professional Guide to Qualifying for Real Estate Using Assets, Not Income

The purpose of *The Asset-Based Mortgage Mastery Series* is to give borrowers, investors, and financial professionals the same strategies used by banks, private lenders, and institutional investors—translated into clear, practical guidance that can be applied in real life. This series is designed to take you from foundational understanding to advanced mastery of how to qualify for, structure, and scale real estate financing using assets instead of traditional income.

Each book builds on the last. You are not just learning how to get approved—you are learning how to think, structure, and operate like the institutions that control capital.

Book 1 — Asset-Based Mortgage Loan Fundamentals

This book gives you the foundation. You will understand how asset-based mortgage loans work, how asset depletion is calculated, how lenders evaluate risk, and why income is no longer the only path to qualification. This is where you shift your mindset from income-based borrowing to asset-based strategy.

Book 2 — Retirement Asset Mortgage Qualification

This book focuses on using retirement accounts such as 401(k)s, IRAs, and investment portfolios to qualify for mortgage loans. You will learn how lenders evaluate retirement assets, how to access them strategically, and how to structure your finances to qualify without disrupting long-term retirement growth.

Book 3 — High-Net-Worth Asset-Based Mortgage Strategies

This book is designed for borrowers with significant assets who want to optimize leverage, preserve liquidity, and structure large or complex transactions. You will learn how wealthy borrowers qualify without traditional income and how to position assets for maximum efficiency and control.

Book 4 — Primary Residence Asset-Based Mortgage Loans

This book shows you how to purchase or refinance your primary home using assets instead of income. You will learn how to structure down payments, reserves, and loan options to maximize flexibility while maintaining long-term financial stability.

Book 5 — Investment Property Asset-Based Mortgage Loans

This book focuses on building a real estate portfolio using asset-based lending. You will learn how to qualify for multiple properties, integrate rental income, manage reserves, and scale your investments without being limited by income.

Book 6 — Securities-Based Mortgage Lending Strategies

This book explores how to use stocks, bonds, and brokerage accounts to secure financing. You will learn how to leverage investment portfolios without liquidating them, preserving growth while accessing capital for real estate opportunities.

Book 7 — Foreign National Asset-Based Mortgage Loans

This book explains how international buyers can qualify for U.S. real estate using global assets. You will learn how lenders evaluate foreign income and assets, and how to structure deals across borders with confidence.

Book 8 — Jumbo Asset-Based Mortgage Loans

This book focuses on financing high-value and luxury properties. You will learn how to structure large loan amounts, meet stricter guidelines, and position assets to qualify for jumbo financing without traditional income.

Book 9 — Asset-Based Mortgage Refinancing & Equity Access

This book teaches you how to unlock equity from existing properties using asset-based strategies. You will learn how to refinance without income, access liquidity, and use your equity to fund new investments or opportunities.

Book 10 — Advanced Asset-Based Mortgage Structuring

This book brings everything together. You will learn how to engineer approvals, layer assets, sequence transactions, and create sophisticated financing strategies that maximize flexibility, control, and long-term growth.

This series is designed to move you step-by-step from understanding to execution to mastery. By the end, you will not just know how to qualify for loans—you will understand how to control capital, structure wealth, and build a financial system that works for you long-term.

Educational & Financial Disclaimer

The *Asset-Based Mortgage Mastery Series* is intended for educational and informational purposes only. The content provided throughout this series is designed to help readers better understand asset-based mortgage lending, real estate financing strategies, and financial structuring concepts. It is not intended to be, and should not be interpreted as, financial, legal, tax, investment, or mortgage advice.

Joseph G. Correa and Live Stronger Faster are not acting as your personal financial advisor, attorney, accountant, or licensed mortgage professional in any jurisdiction through this publication. All information is presented in a general format and may not apply to your specific financial situation, goals, or circumstances. Readers are strongly encouraged to consult with qualified professionals—including licensed mortgage brokers, financial advisors, tax professionals, and attorneys—before making any financial or real estate decisions.

Mortgage lending guidelines, underwriting standards, and loan program availability vary by lender, location, and over time. Asset-based mortgage programs, including asset depletion loans and non-qualified mortgage (Non-QM) products, are subject to change without notice. The examples, strategies, and scenarios presented in this series are for illustration purposes only and do not guarantee approval, specific loan terms, or financial outcomes. Individual results will vary based on credit profile, asset structure, property type, market conditions, and lender requirements.

Real estate investing and the use of leverage involve risk. Property values can fluctuate, interest rates can change, and market conditions may impact both income and asset performance. While asset-based lending provides flexibility, it also requires careful planning, risk management, and financial discipline. Readers are responsible for evaluating their own risk tolerance and making decisions that align with their long-term financial goals.

Any references to potential income, returns, cash flow, or financial growth are not guarantees or promises of performance. These outcomes depend on multiple factors beyond the control of the author and publisher, including economic conditions, market trends, borrower decisions, and lender policies.

The author and publisher make no representations or warranties regarding the accuracy, completeness, or reliability of the information contained in this series. While every effort has been made to provide accurate and up-to-date information, errors or omissions may occur. The author and publisher disclaim any liability for losses, damages, or consequences resulting from the use or misuse of the information provided.

By reading this series, you acknowledge that you are solely responsible for your financial decisions and actions. The purpose of this content is to provide knowledge, perspective, and strategic insight—not to replace professional advice or guarantee specific outcomes.

Use this information as a guide, not a substitute for professional consultation, and always make decisions based on your individual financial situation, goals, and risk tolerance.

Risk Disclosure

The *Asset-Based Mortgage Mastery Series* discusses financial strategies involving real estate, lending, leverage, and asset-based qualification methods. These strategies involve inherent risks, and it is important that all readers fully understand and accept these risks before applying any concepts presented in this series.

Real estate markets are subject to fluctuation. Property values may rise or fall due to economic conditions, interest rate changes, local market dynamics, or unforeseen events. There is no guarantee that any property will appreciate in value or generate consistent income. Investments in real estate may result in financial loss.

The use of leverage, including mortgage financing and asset-based lending, increases both potential returns and potential risks. Borrowing against assets or property can amplify losses if market conditions change or if income from investments does not perform as expected. Failure to meet loan obligations may result in foreclosure, loss of property, or damage to credit.

Asset-based mortgage lending relies on the valuation and accessibility of financial assets. Investment accounts, retirement funds, and other assets may fluctuate in value due to market volatility. A decline in asset value may impact a borrower's financial position, liquidity, and ability to refinance or secure additional financing.

Interest rates may change over time, particularly with adjustable-rate or interest-only loan structures. Rising interest rates can increase monthly payments, reduce cash flow, and affect long-term affordability. Borrowers must be prepared for potential payment increases and plan accordingly.

Liquidity risk is another important consideration. While asset-based lending allows borrowers to qualify using assets, those assets may be tied up in investments or subject to penalties or restrictions. In times of financial stress, accessing funds may not be as immediate or favorable as expected.

Rental income and investment returns are not guaranteed. Vacancy, tenant issues, maintenance costs, property management expenses, and market conditions can all impact cash flow. Relying on projected income without accounting for these variables can create financial strain.

Refinancing and equity access strategies depend on market conditions, property values, and lender guidelines. There is no assurance that refinancing will be available in the future or that favorable terms will be offered. Changes in lending standards or economic conditions may limit access to capital.

Private lending, capital recycling, and advanced financial strategies discussed in this series involve additional layers of risk, including borrower default, insufficient collateral, and market uncertainty. These strategies require careful due diligence and risk management.

Tax laws and regulations may change over time, affecting the benefits of certain strategies such as depreciation, capital gains deferral, or asset structuring. Readers should consult with qualified tax professionals to understand how these changes may impact their financial plans.

All financial decisions involve risk, and past performance or examples presented in this series do not guarantee future results. The scenarios and illustrations provided are for educational purposes only and may not reflect actual outcomes. Individual results will vary based on personal circumstances, market conditions, and execution.

By using the information in this series, you acknowledge that you understand the risks involved and accept full responsibility for your financial decisions. The author and publisher are not liable for any losses, damages, or outcomes resulting from the application of the concepts discussed.

It is essential to approach asset-based lending and real estate investing with careful planning, professional guidance, and a clear understanding of your financial goals and risk tolerance.

www.ingramcontent.com/pod-product-compliance
Lightning Source LLC
LaVergne TN
LVHW022222200926
848481LV00006B/2078